THE ONLY CHILD

THE ONLY CHILD

A Guide for Parents and Only Children of All Ages

NORMA E. CUTTS, Ph.D.
and
NICHOLAS MOSELEY, Ph.D.

FOUNDED 1838

GPPS

G. P. Putnam's Sons, New York

Foreword and Acknowledgments

THE original materials on which this book is based come from five sources: 258 case histories of only children of all ages; an analysis of the vital statistics of the alumnae of Mount Holyoke and of Vassar through the classes of 1937; studies of the occupational and marital records of (a) the 127 Onlies in these classes at Mount Holyoke who were daughters of Mount Holyoke alumnae, (b) the 55 Onlies in these classes at Vassar who were daughters of Vassar alumnae, and (c) the 34 Onlies in the Yale class of 1919; detailed school records and test scores, compiled by psychological examiners, of 24 elementary- and secondary-school students; and miscellaneous reports on Onlies by parents, teachers, and Onlies themselves which we have culled from the materials we collected for our books *Practical School Discipline and Mental Hygiene, Better Home Discipline,* and *Bright Children.* We have also made a series of statistical checks to determine the probable proportions of Onlies in groups with various backgrounds.

Two hundred and eleven of our case histories are of adults, and the other 47 of young people who have not yet finished their education. The histories are based on notes of interviews with individual Onlies or their parents, occasionally supplemented by reports from their associates and acquaintances. We encouraged all concerned to talk freely and gave assurance of anonymity. In each case we tried to ascertain why the only child was an Only, what advantages and disadvantages were seen in Onliness, what experiences had been helpful, and what, if anything, might well have been managed differently.

We found nearly everyone whom we interviewed eager to cooperate. Many of our best cases were volunteered by people who had heard of the work we were doing. As a result, we obtained a great deal of practical information about how parents help Onlies to develop healthy personalities, what are the dangers to be avoided, and what safeguards are efficacious.

Before we began our own research, psychologists, psychiatrists, and sociologists had written more than two hundred articles on only children. All but three of these studies deal primarily with young children. Almost all were written for professional workers and published in professional magazines. They are in Czech, Dutch, French, German, Greek, Italian, and Russian as well as English. The only child may not be a problem to his parents but he certainly is to scholars.

As far as we know, the only book on Onlies is *Het Eenige Kind,* by the Dutch psychiatrist Dr. D. Arn. van Krevelen, published in 1946 by Erven J. Bijleveld in Utrecht. Van Krevelen studied only children in the lower elementary grades of schools in Holland and also among the children referred to mental-hygiene clinics. Despite the differences between wartime Holland and postwar America, we have found van Krevelen's work both illuminating and suggestive, and we stand in debt to him.

Albert A. Campbell's article "The Personality Adjustments of Only Children" (*Psychological Bulletin,* Vol. XXXI, No. 3, March 1934, pp. 193-203) is a very useful summary of the facts and opinions contained in earlier research.

Maternal Overprotection, by David M. Levy, M.D. (Fourth Printing, Columbia University Press, New York, 1950), is the standard work in a field of special interest to the parents of only children. Levy studied twenty severe cases of maternal overprotection among the children referred to the Institute for Child Guidance in New York. Ten of these children were only children at the time of their referral. Most of the cases were followed for eleven years. The book contains a frank appraisal of the methods of treatment employed and the results.

The *Smith College Studies in Social Work* contain a number of monographs about one or another of the situations which we discuss. Many of the studies were written under Levy's direction.

The studies in child development made by Dr. Arnold Gesell and his associates in the Yale Institute of Human Relations and the Gesell Institute have become so much a part of psychological knowledge that it is easy to take them for granted. We have tried to acknowledge the contributions they have made to our work, but we realize these are general as well as specific. Children's problems are essentially problems of development. Gesell has made the solutions of these problems infinitely easier than they would have been twenty-five years ago.

We have used many other books and articles to back up various conclusions or to present divergent opinions. In each case we have tried to cite the author by name.

The editors of *Parents Magazine* have kindly permitted us to use materials from an article, "When Should Your Child Stay Alone?" which we wrote for their magazine.

Mrs. Virginia Carrick, associate editor of G. P. Putnam's Sons and herself the mother of an Only, has given our work all the help and attention that any *Only Child* might crave. Mr. Charles Cutts, who was raised as an Only and is the father of an Only, has given us the benefit of the wisdom and experience of his eighty-seven years. Mrs. Nicholas Moseley, the daughter of an Only, has criticized both our style and our conclusions with admirable objectivity. She has typed and retyped the manuscript and supervised our preparation of the index. The reader, the publisher, and the authors all owe her thanks.

Contents

THE ONLY CHILD

I.

On Being an Only Child

IF you are an only child or the parent of one, you have plenty of company.

In the United States as a whole, about one couple in six of all those who ever have a child has just one. About one child in twenty is an only child. These are minimum figures. In some groups of well-educated, native, white city-dwellers, one couple in three never has more than one child, and one adult in ten is an Only.

These figures are for absolute Onlies, that is, those who never had a living brother or sister and whose mothers are past the age of childbearing. Of course every oldest child is an only child for a longer or shorter period. Add the number of people who were raised as only children because they were much older or much younger than the other children in the family or because they were left alone by the death of another child, and you see what a legion of Onlies there is.

You can make these figures come alive if you will count the Onlies in any gathering. If you are at a party with fifteen people, you are quite likely to find one or two Onlies present. The laws of chance dictate that in some groups there will be none, in others more than you expect. But by and large every group, be it a kindergarten class or a cocktail party, a get-together of a company's salesmen or a meeting of management, will have a few Onlies present.

3

Famous Onlies

Onlies have become leaders in every field. Franklin D. Roosevelt in government, Edsel Ford in industry, and Arthur T. Hadley in education are among the famous American Onlies. Charles Augustus Lindbergh was raised as an Only. We all owe happy hours to Hans Christian Andersen and Robert Louis Stevenson, both Onlies. And there are famous parents of only children. President Eisenhower has an only son, and ex-President Truman an only daughter.

The Popular Opinion of Onlies

A Gallup poll conducted in 1950 asked a cross section of voters: "Do you think being an only child is an advantage or disadvantage?" The replies were separated into two groups, those from Onlies (10 per cent) and all others. Of the Onlies, 25 per cent said being an only child was an advantage, 60 per cent a disadvantage, and 15 per cent didn't know. Of the non-Onlies questioned, 20 per cent said being an only child was an advantage, 73 per cent a disadvantage, and 7 per cent didn't know. Other polls and surveys have shown that less than one per cent of American married couples think that the one-child family is ideal. One study, *Social and Psychological Factors Affecting Fertility* (the Milbank Fund survey of Indianapolis), showed that "not wanting an Only" is one of the most important reasons given by parents for having a second child. And another frequently mentioned reason is the first child's desire to have a baby brother or sister.

We have regularly asked the Onlies whom we interviewed how they had felt about being only children when they were young. A healthily large number say they never gave the matter much if any thought, though there were times when they would have liked a brother or sister to do things with. A very few say they positively liked being an only child. The great majority say they envied their friends who had brothers and sisters. They remember how lonely they often felt. Some say they were spoiled, and some say they were so protected that they were never allowed to do the things which their friends enjoyed.

Two bright teen-agers, writing anonymous essays on the subject, "My Major Problem," express what many young people feel. A boy says, "I am an only child and I will admit I am spoiled. I hate it this way and I wish I had a brother or sister." A girl, who feels hurt because her friends think she is conceited, says, "I have always longed for a brother or sister and I think that may be part of it. It is not possible, however, that I will ever have one." One 6-year-old girl so longs for brothers and sisters that she calls her dolls "Brother Tim" and "Sister Helen." Another, found leaving sugar lumps on the sill of an open window, explained that she was trying to attract a new baby to the family.

Even the Onlies who cannot remember being bothered by Onliness are inclined to state emphatically that they wouldn't have an only child if they could help it. One adult, an Only herself, tells how determined she was not to have an Only. She had a difficult time with the birth of number one. Then, despite her husband's pleadings and her doctor's advice, she continued to try to have another child. After three miscarriages, she finally had a second son, and says, "I'm glad I didn't give up—and the boys are glad, too."

The Fallacy

It must be pointed out that popular opinion is often fallacious. Like the results of some investigations into Onliness, popular opinion may depend on false generalizations and inadequate comparisons. A person sees someone he knows to be an Only act selfishly or hears him speak conceitedly and says, "Just like an only child." This judgment ignores alike all the selfish, conceited non-Onlies and all the generous, thoughtful Onlies. It ignores the whole problem of the specific causes of the behavior in question and whether or not these causes arise from Onliness.

An elementary-school principal, one of the best we know, was talking about her difficulties with an only child in the school: "Just like an Only! They're all like that." There and then we challenged her to spot the other Onlies in the school. She missed twenty-five out of thirty. Though one of us is an Only who blames her real and fancied shortcomings on her Onliness, and though both of us have been studying the characteristics of Onlies for some years, we are not able to tell whether people we meet and talk with are Onlies. We play a game, "Spot the Only," and must admit that our successes are largely a matter of luck.

Prior Research

Onliness has been the subject of more than two hundred special investigations. We shall have occasion to refer to several of these again and again in this book. Unfortunately, the overall results are not conclusive. There have been unwarranted generalizations in both directions. Some scholars have found that *on the average* the only children whom they studied were superior in one or several character traits or behavior habits. Others have found that *on the average* they were inferior. In both cases the conclusion has too often been that all only children were like the average of only children in the group under investigation. The truth is that, just as with all children, some Onlies are superior, some average, and some below average. Unbiased reading of all the studies makes it clear that there are as great individual differences among only children as there are among all children and that Onlies are not necessarily either good or bad.

Current Expert Opinion

James H. S. Bossard, a professor of sociology at the University of Pennsylvania and the director of the William Carter Foundation, discusses only children in his books *The Sociology of Child Development* and *Parent and Child*. He distinguishes between the popular and the scientific points of view. Popular opinion generalizes that only children are spoiled and sensitive. The scientist thinks in terms of causative factors: what is there in the circumstances of Onliness which may cause good or bad results? Bossard reasons that "the only child lacks the things that siblings give each other," notably the sense of security and conviction of support which are the basis of mental hygiene. Siblings, he says, force each other to keep in touch with reality. They provide intimate play and competition within the family. They save each other from too close association with their parents and from receiving too much attention from their parents. The only child's parents tend to be overanxious about his health, to overemphasize minor problems and minor achievements, and to introduce him to adult activities too soon. Their emotional demands "converge on the only child." "Small families provide a poor kind of training" for adult life in a large plant or office building with thousands of workers, or in an army of millions of men, where the Only will be "a single cog in a huge machine, a role diametrically the opposite of that he enjoyed in the small family."

But, Bossard says, the only child has certain distinct advantages. Ordinarily his economic position is better. His parents have more time to devote to supervision and guidance. They show in many ways that they expect much of him, and so hold him up to making the most of himself.

Dr. William Menninger, of the Menninger Foundation,

in an outline for a lecture on the "Psychology of the Only Child," starts with, "Obvious facts: no sibling competition (or rivalry); undivided parental investment." He says that the reason for the child's being an Only, e.g., the death of a parent or divorce before a second child is conceived, may have an adverse effect. But, he says, parents who recognize handicaps can take specific steps to overcome them.

The Advantages of Onliness

Onlies, being human, are quite likely to think more of the disadvantages than of the advantages of their state. But in many cases the advantages are very real.

As Bossard points out, the only child is usually favored economically. His parents can afford to spend more on him than they could if they had to spread their income to supply the needs of several children. Too much money may be a bad thing, but a sufficiency wisely spent certainly helps: it makes it possible to give the child the best medical care, food, clothing (no hand-me-downs!), a room of his own, and a good education. How being an Only affects length of schooling is shown by our study of the Onlies in one Yale class. A significantly larger proportion of Onlies than of non-Onlies were awarded the B.A. degree, and, of these B.A.'s, a somewhat larger proportion of Onlies than of non-Onlies took additional academic and scientific degrees. (See Chapter XIV.)

The academic achievements of Onlies raise the question as to whether the only child is likely to have a higher IQ than the non-Only. Two studies are of marked interest here. The Royal Commission on Population in 1947 gave intelligence tests to the 70,805 11-year-old children in Scotland. (The Scots are thorough people!) The report states, "The phenomenon of decreasing average score with increasing size of family, evident in 1933, is fully confirmed beyond all possible doubt." The 7,824 only children had the highest *average* IQ. Though their average was very slightly above that of the 15,971 children with one sibling, it was one seventh above that of the children from four-child families and one sixth above that of the children from eight-child families. Ann Ward found that the *average* IQ of 100 only children referred to certain clinics was 109.8, compared with 103.3 for the *average* of all children referred to the same clinics.

Parents should not be complacent about these figures. In the first place they are averages. There are dull and defective children as well as bright children among Onlies. The IQ is based on tests in which only children perhaps have an advantage since their closer association with adults may make them "old for their years." Many Onlies are the offspring of couples whose superior social and economic status reflects ability which their children presumably inherit. But, regardless of the explanation, the fact remains that Onlies as a group are in a favored position educationally speaking.

The greatest asset which a growing child can have is a sense that he is loved wholeheartedly by his parents. The good adjustment which the vast majority of Onlies achieve seems to us to be due in no small measure to the very fact that they grew up sure of their parents' love. The only child, just because he has no brothers and sisters who might be loved more than he, is in a secure position. A well-adjusted, attractive, 17-year-old girl, when we asked her how she felt about being an Only, summed up the situation succinctly: "I like it." "Why?" "No competition."

Our Adult Onlies

It has always seemed to us that the crucial question about Onliness was what sort of adults individuals who were raised as only children turned out to be. We believe that we have studied more adult Onlies than any other investigator

has. In reviewing their case histories, we have asked ourselves five questions: Was this Only's education in line with
his abilities and opportunities? Has he to date made a success of his business or professional life? Has he a happy family life? Has he good friends and a pleasant social life? Is
he taking an active part in community life and carrying his
full share of public duties?

We do not find that Onlies *as a group* constitute an unusual class of people. Among our Onlies, just as among our
acquaintances in general, are some who have been outstand-
ingly successful and some who might be called failures. The
great majority are leading normal lives, with all this implies
in the way of achievement and disappointment, of sorrow
and of joy.

If this were the whole story, we should stop here. But we
are not stopping. We are going on to write a whole book
because we have found in our case histories a considerable
number of problems, personal or circumstantial or both,
which seem logically connected with Onliness. We see how
parents, if they had given more consideration to the circumstances connected with Onliness, might have saved some
individuals a great deal of pain and trouble. We do not
mean that more only children than non-Onlies have difficulties. In the course of growing up, all children meet difficulties, the number and the seriousness of which depend
not on the child's being oldest or youngest or only but on
many circumstances in the life of the individual. But just
as the youngest children owe some of their difficulties to being the youngest, and the oldest to being the oldest, so only
children owe some of their struggles to being Onlies. Moreover, many of our case histories show in detail steps which
parents and only children themselves have taken which
have led to fortunate results. This is practical advice based
on experience, and we think it should be passed on.

II.

Why Some Parents Behave As They Do

A CAREFUL study of the case history of an Only who is in difficulties of any kind invariably discloses that the cause is not simply Onliness as such. There are always complicating factors. Many of these are also found in the backgrounds of non-Onlies, but because the family troubles and parental shortcomings "converge on the only child," the Only who is placed in adverse circumstances may be more handicapped than the non-Only in similar circumstances.

Inexperience

Many only children undoubtedly suffer because their parents are inexperienced. Even parents who were themselves brought up in large families may not know or remember what a baby is like. Parents from small families have still less of a chance. As Mrs. Sidonie Matsner Gruenberg of the Child Study Association points out ("Changing Conceptions of the Family," *Annals of the American Academy of Political and Social Science,* May 1947), many small American families are the second or third in a series of small families; there are few experienced relatives to call upon for help. She remarks that "the parents of an only child have no margin of error." So, trusted with a live baby that seems ever so much more fragile than the most delicate doll, the parents are afraid. They worry and tense up and make the never-easy job of caring for a baby harder and harder. Their anxiety and their fatigue are quickly reflected by the baby, and so a vicious circle starts.

The modern parent turns to books and magazines dealing with child care as a remedy for inexperience and as a supplement to the advice given by the doctor. The overall result is good. Baby bibles are certainly helping to cut down the mortality rate. Another service which these books render is the reassurance they give to parents by showing that the great majority of babies in the world behave, and misbehave, just like theirs. Fifty members of a Mothers Club, who told us what help they got from books, placed reassurance first, and advice to relax and take it easy in toilet training second.

But a goodly number of parents, instead of being reassured by what they read, are upset by it. They fail to heed what the experts say about individual differences and go into a dither because their child is not just like the one in the book. Sometimes they jump at conclusions.

One mother of a 4-year-old Only was reading the "Gradient of Elimination" in *The Child from Five to Ten* by Arnold Gesell and Frances L. Ilg. She saw, "4 years. Bowel. This function has become a private affair." Her son still needed help with wiping. Was he defective? Luckily, she cast her eye down the page and saw, "5 Years. Bowel. . . . Many still need help with wiping."

There are plenty of parents who are gravely upset by misunderstandings as simple as this, and they often give their first child a bad time. If a second comes along with reasonable promptness, they take in their stride matters that made them run to call the doctor for the first. They know now that children have a way of surviving. They face their problems calmly and with confidence. The resulting peace is good for everyone, including the older child, though there may still be some truth in the idea that first children tend to grow up tense and overactive. Their parents relax too late.

For the Only there is no automatic relief from parental anxieties. The parents must work deliberately for wide knowledge and then cultivate a sense of humor in applying it. They should by all means read many books and articles on child care, especially if they are able to laugh at the disagreements of the experts. They should talk over together what they read, and air their doubts. Above all they should belong to a Parents Club—at the very least the mother should belong to a Mothers Club—and take every chance they can get to compare notes on child care with other parents.

The Way the Parents Were Brought Up

Some of our parents of Onlies are quick to attribute their ideas about child care to their own experience as children. This is excellent when it results in the parents' striving to give the only child the kind of experience which they remember enjoying with brothers and sisters. One mother says, "I remember how my sister and I used to support each other against our parents. So when Sally says, 'All the other kids do it,' I take her seriously and bend over backwards to let her have her way." A father, who delighted in his own family's gathering of the clan at Thanksgiving, makes a considerable sacrifice of time and money to take his son to the annual family dinner in a distant city.

Reactions against the way the parent was brought up are also a strong and evident influence in the bringing up of Onlies. Again, this may be all to the good. A parent who was never allowed any freedom may build his child's independence wisely and well. But it is very easy to use past experience as an excuse for a course that is really being steered to suit oneself. We have examples of families who are bringing up children in the city because one of the parents hated his childhood on a farm, and *vice versa*. There are many cases of parents who, feeling they were brought up too strictly, use this as an excuse to overindulge an only child.

Rationalization by the parents of their attitudes and methods as outcomes of their own upbringing is easier for an outsider to detect than for the parents themselves. The clue is to consider whether the situations are really parallel. One mother, brought up in New York City but now living in a friendly semicountry suburb, refuses to let her son go anywhere or do anything by himself. Her excuse is, "My parents never let me play in Central Park alone."

Psychiatrists stress the fact that childhood experiences may control adult behavior without the adult's being in the least conscious of *why* he is behaving as he does. He may even disapprove of his own behavior but be compelled to continue in it. He may have a thousand reasons, none of them correct, for what he does. Dr. David Levy places lack of parental affection first among the parent's childhood experiences which force a parent to overprotect his child. Dr. D. Arn. van Krevelen speaks of the narcissistic parent who sees himself in the child and praises the child indiscriminately as a means of praising himself. Many psychiatrists of the Freudian school trace parental behavior to experiences in the parent's early childhood and particularly to experiences connected with "psychosexual" development. Other past experiences which are said to control parental attitudes without the parent's being conscious of the cause include sibling rivalry, resentment of authoritarian domination, many kinds of fears, and many kinds of failures. Our case histories include examples of the ill effects of most of these influences. For example, one of our Onlies is dangerously timid. The immediate cause of his trouble is apparently his father's tendency to dominate. But an examination of the family history indicates that the father's dominance goes back to an intense rivalry with an older brother for his father's—our Only's grandfather's—affection.

Overage Parents

A very large number of only children are born after their parents are 30. This is true of 53 per cent of our 107 Onlies whose case histories show their parents' ages. It is also true of the 459 only children born to all the mothers who graduated from Vassar between 1867 and 1914. Eighteen per cent of our group and 25 per cent of the Vassar group were born when their parents were 35 years old or older. In contrast, the "statistically average" mother in the United States bears her *last* child by the age of 27. College graduates are likely to marry late and bear children later than the average. But of a group of graduates of Vassar with more than one child, 50 per cent had their first child by the age of 26, and less than 5 per cent of all their children were born after the age of 35.

There is no doubt that much Onliness is due to late marriage and a considerable amount to conception just before the menopause. But here we are less concerned with causes than with the effects on children of having overage parents. In his book *Parent and Child*, Bossard has a chapter, "Children of Overage Parents," in which he analyzes the problem, reviews the literature, and cites examples from 17 case histories of individuals who are thirty-five years or more younger than their parents. Bossard pictures the physical, psychosocial, and cultural problems that are posed by a wide age differential. Overage parents are likely to die or become dependent on the child before the child is established in life and able to assume the responsibility. Older parents are different from the parents of most of the child's playmates, and this may add to his feelings of insecurity. The difference in attitudes between generations, especially in this era of rapid change, increases as the differential be-

tween parent and child increases. Older parents are likely
to be set in their ways, to be overprotective, and unsympathetic. Age is conservative, youth experimental. The
possible advantages, according to Bossard, are that
"many overage parents are well situated economically and
give their children unusual opportunities for development"
and that the parents may have established themselves in
positions of leadership which make their children proud of
them.

Our case histories show a large number of Onlies who are
successful despite having been born to parents in the thir-
ties. There are, for example, a college president, a leading
research chemist, a prominent doctor, and a wealthy
banker, all of whom are happily married as well as successful in their chosen fields. Women show parallel examples of
successful careers in teaching, in business, and as mothers.
At the same time, our case histories of late-born children
do emphasize the difficulties. The histories include an unusually large number of orphans and of children who have
had to sacrifice marriage or a chosen career or both to care
for elderly and failing parents.

People who marry late or have a child after years of waiting are fortunate in having a child of their own. They must,
however, recognize that the age differential aggravates the
handicaps which an only child suffers, and that these increase as time goes by. Though parents cannot keep themselves young, they can plan to let their child be young.

Delayed Conception

The couple who very much want children but continue
childless while their friends and neighbors succeed, suffer
keen frustration. Conception after a long wait institutes a
period of acute anxiety. When the child is finally carried
to term and born healthy and happy and, to the parents'

eyes, beautiful, there is no greater treasure in the world. The treasure is to be guarded, not like one of a bunch of grapes but as a pearl beyond price. Nothing is too hard for the parents, and nothing too good for the child. All of which often adds up to overprotection and overindulgence.

Miscarriages complicate the emotional picture. A child born after a series of miscarriages is doubly treasured because the parents can't help fearing that a tendency to miscarry will prevent the birth of a second child. A subsequent miscarriage confirms this fear. But if the sex of the fetus is determined and happens to be preferred to that of the first child, there may be dangerous feelings of regret —"If it could have been the other way"—and so of rejection and ultimately of guilt. When there can be no second child, because of the age of the mother, a hysterectomy, or the death of the mother or father, all the anxieties and all the handicaps to a normal rearing are more than doubled.

Our case histories are full of examples of children born after long waits, after miscarriages, and in births so difficult that no other child was possible. Some of these Onlies have had an extremely hard time learning to adjust, apparently because their parents have overprotected them. A few have failed to adjust. A goodly number have been well brought up and are happy, useful citizens and parents. For example, one young lawyer, now 35, was born when his mother was 26 and had been married five years. She hemorrhaged so severely that her life was despaired of, and she knew she could have no more children. She set out, as she says, to do everything she could to make her son's life normal. She made her house the center of his crowd. She encouraged him in his athletics. She sent him away to camp when he was young and to a good preparatory school and one of the best colleges. She had him pay long visits to his grandparents. He enlisted on the day after Pearl Harbor and had a long combat record as an Air Force pilot. He married immediately after the war and is now doing well in his profession and as the father of three children.

Feelings of Guilt

The traditional disparagement of the only child makes some parents feel guilty about having an Only. We see evidences of this in parents who have deliberately planned to have one child for economic reasons and then accuse themselves of being selfish. We see it even more often in mothers who for one reason or another are physically incapable of having another baby. They blame themselves for their inability to give their child the advantages of a large family.

The discrepancy between the small number of couples who say they think the one-child family is the most desirable and the far larger number who actually have just one child suggests that many parents may wonder if they are living up to their ideals.

Guilt over being the parent of an Only manifests itself in several ways. There is likely to be an extreme touchiness on the subject. This may make it difficult for the parent to follow Menninger's advice to "recognize the handicaps and take specific steps to overcome them," though it has been our experience during interviews that the touchiest parents very quickly come round to welcoming a chance to talk about their problems. For example, one mother who greeted us with the remark, "There's entirely too much talk about Onlies," was soon deep in discussing the very concrete problem of how not to be a burden on her son as she grew older.

More serious is the guilt-inspired feeling that the parent must make up to the Only for his being an Only. This would be all to the good if the parent remained objective, planned constructively, and acted accordingly. But a guilty conscience, whether it is due to rejection or regret, is not conducive to objectivity. The net result is likely to be unthinking indulgence and overprotection.

Perhaps the guilt-ridden parent can find comfort in realizing how mistakenly romantic the idea of the large family may be. Just as the unmarried spinster looks on matrimony as the promised land and blindly ignores matters like diapers and divorce, so the parents of an Only, and Onlies themselves, do not consider how unpleasant fights between children can be. One Only, the parent of two children, says, "I grew up being sure that it was a tragedy to be an Only. Now my boys fight all the time, and I'm sure two is not the right answer."

Rejection

So much is said about only children being overindulged and overprotected that it is hard to think of an only child being unwanted and unloved, or, to use the psychological term, rejected. Yet Dr. Sophie Sloonan, studying 62 cases of clear rejection among children who were being treated at a Chicago clinic, found that 17 (27.4 per cent) were only children.

There are many reasons why an only child may be rejected. Luckily they do not usually operate. A baby has his own ways of winning love.

A couple may not want to have any children, or "at least not yet." The Milbank Fund survey of 1445 Indianapolis couples showed that of 365 only children, 54, or 14.8 per cent, were unwanted at the time of conception. The couples covered by this section of the survey were definitely planning their families. These 54 had "accidents."

A baby, though wanted, may disappoint one or both parents by being of the "wrong" sex. Sloonan says that 16 per cent of the children in her study of rejection were rejected because the parents were disappointed by the child's sex.

On the other hand, the Indianapolis survey indicated that such disappointment is not as great a factor in rejection as has sometimes been supposed. About half the women and two fifths of the men had had no prior preference for one sex or another in their Only. A mere 11 per cent said they still wished the child were of the opposite sex. Of those planning another child, less than 6 per cent gave dissatisfaction with the sex of the first as a reason.

A more common cause of rejection is that the psychologically immature parent finds the baby more of a nuisance or more of a stubborn individual than the parent had bargained for. The child is a drag on life, messy, dirty, disobedient. One half of Sloonan's rejecting mothers were "compulsive perfectionists who would tolerate nothing but perfect behavior."

Marital discord is a frequent cause of both Onliness and rejection. Parents who disagree about having a baby, those who have a baby in a vain attempt to save a marriage, and those who stay married for the child's sake, may all end up resenting their only child and not having another. One third of Sloonan's cases are in this category.

The majority of rejecting parents probably never admit to themselves that they do not want their child. They are often not in any way conscious of it. But some parents are frankly aware of the fact of rejection. In that case they are likely to run away from their responsibility. One of our Onlies says, "My parents didn't want me. They got divorced right after I was born and left me with my grandparents. I got married at 18 to escape my grandparents and got divorced myself at 21."

Even when parents sincerely love a child, they may do things which make the child feel rejected. The parents think they are exercising plain common sense. The child thinks they have no sympathy with his troubles. One Only reports that her mother was never sympathetic enough. "If she was going out and I had a headache, she'd always say, 'Oh, it'll be over by bedtime,' and go along. As a result I am much too self-reliant." It's better to humor a psychological headache once in a while than to have a child think you do not love him.

And, at least, parents of an Only are spared the suffering of the parents of several children who read some of the popular accounts of the dangers of playing favorites. The Only's parents can like and love their child without fear of being unfair.

III.

Misguided Affection

CHILD psychologists agree unanimously that a child needs to feel sure of his parents' love and secure in the knowledge that they will protect him. But all of the research on only children discloses the dangers of parents' concentrating affection on the child and overprotecting him. Parents, like tightrope walkers, must be sure never to lean too far to one side or the other. They must love, but not to excess. They must protect, but not overprotect. Luckily, like the expert performer, they gain confidence with time.

Concentrated Emotion

There is really no such thing as loving a child too much, but one can certainly manifest that love unwisely and let it exercise a dangerous control over one's own actions.

In the normal course of events the manifestations of parental love change as a child develops. There is less physical contact and less direct care. Protection gives way to loving pride in the child's ability to do things for himself. The will to protect is no less, but it is held in restraint.

When a couple have a second child they are more than ready to encourage the first to act independently. The new baby needs the loving care that the older one has had, and there just is not time to give the same care to both. The older child is pushed out of the nest and must begin to exercise the ability to care for himself which his physical and mental development have provided.

The only child likewise progresses physically and mentally. This development may, and we think usually does, help the parents adjust the expression of their love to his changing needs. After all, there are a great many things that a two-year-old can do for himself that a mother is just as glad to leave to him. There is danger, however, that the parents, with their love focused as it is on the one child, will try to keep him from moving ahead.

Love is like sunshine. If love floods a house there is an atmosphere of cheer and well-being. But just as the sun's rays when concentrated through a magnifying glass may cause a conflagration that lays waste the home, so love that is too concentrated may destroy.

Parents of an only child are free to concentrate not only their love and attention but their energy and anxiety on him. In fact, all four are usually combined. What the results can be is shown by the case of one of our 14-year-old Onlies.

Mary is the daughter of fairly well-to-do American parents. She was born after a four-year wait and two months prematurely. She weighed only three pounds and had to be kept in a specially heated room. Her mother later had several miscarriages and, when Mary was 6, gave birth to another seven-months baby, who died at birth. Mary has always been thin and undersized, and the parents are always taking her temperature and calling the doctor. The parents once kept an all-night vigil at her bedside when the doctor had assured them that she was just suffering from a mild cold.

Mary's father is a skilled photographer. Every table in the house supports a framed picture of Mary.

The family lives a few blocks from school, but Mary was not allowed to go and come from school alone until December of her freshman year in high school. In school she has never played with other children. As a young child, in first and second grades, she had frequent temper tantrums and never would join hands with other children in circle games. She is still withdrawing and solitary and often just sits at her desk and does nothing.

Mary at home is a different person. An acquaintance of the family says that there she is just plain nasty. She is disobedient, impertinent, and unwilling to do anything to help. She plays her parents against each other. If they have company, she interrupts constantly and holds the center of the stage. One night, when she had gone to bed after company came, she called down to her father to make her a fried egg sandwich. He broke up the card game, went into the kitchen, made Mary her sandwich, and took it up to her. She then said, so she could be heard, that she didn't want it.

When a psychologist observes intensely concentrated love or anxiety, he is filled with apprehension. Of course, there is always hope that in the natural course of events the parent will disperse his feelings. Sunlight passing through a prism is far prettier than when focused by a burning glass. But many times the parent seems to be driven by some overpowering inner force. It is as though he had some insatiable need for love and security and was compelled to seek them from the child. And this may well be the case. Concentrated love is in reality selfish; though the giver is unconscious of the truth, he gives his love to gain a return.

One frequent manifestation of misguided affection is oversolicitude. A wife reports that her husband is unbearably restless whenever he is not exactly certain what their 7-year-old daughter is doing. When he is home he wants her with him all the time. The daughter has a healthy preference for play with a school friend who lives a few blocks away. She will beg permission to go to the friend's house. The father cannot refuse. But soon after the girl has left he will suggest to his wife that they go over to Plum Lane and see what Sally is doing. They always end by going. If Sally is in sight he will hang around watching her. If she happens to be in the friend's house, he goes into a regular tantrum of fear, convinced that she has lost her way, been kidnaped, or run over. He insists on ringing the bell and satisfying himself.

Strong emotional reaction to an apparent slight from the child indicates overconcentration. One of our adult Onlies remembers visiting his grandmother when he was a child. He can't remember exactly how old he was, but says he must have been very young. When he returned, his mother was waiting for him at the gate. The child brushed past her and went running up the path and around into the garden hunting for his pet spaniel. The mother burst into a paroxysm of tears.

Often the child resists entanglement, and by his resistance helps the parent regain stability. The tendency of an Only (and of every child) to develop away from his parents, to fight to do as much on his own as he can at his stage of development even though he tramples on parental feelings, is not utter selfishness. Rather it is the saving grace in the situation. Parents must be weaned emotionally from the child just as the child must be weaned from the breast. Sometimes they need the child's help.

Family Triangles

Some families seem to outsiders to be an equilateral, firmly closed triangle. They do everything they can together and exclude relatives, neighbors, and the child's schoolmates.

Even when families seem to present a united front, intimate acquaintance is likely to disclose a pairing off within the family. Fathers seem most likely to pair with daughters, and mothers with sons, but father-son and mother-daughter combinations are not unusual. Whatever the combination, both sides are quick with explanations. One of our Onlies says, "Daddy and I do play a lot of tennis together, but

Mother doesn't like tennis." The mother says, "I really prefer to watch." But she was a good player before her daughter was born and still enjoys playing with her friends.

When a parent monopolizes a child of the opposite sex, the child runs a twofold risk. He may, as the Freudians say, have great difficulty in identifying properly and in resolving his Oedipus complex.

Identification, in effect, means that the individual models himself on a given person, usually the parent of the same sex. Identification, in the sense of unconscious imitation of a parent, is obviously common. It is the normal way of learning the role of man or woman in adult life. But either parent may be copied, especially if one is more forceful. Both boys and girls will identify with a mother who, to use an apt phrase, "wears the pants" in a home, and both girls and boys may identify with a father.

An Oedipus complex implies a sexual attachment to the parent of the opposite sex. We shall discuss it more in detail in Chapter XV, "Sex and Marriage." There is no need for parents to be jittery about the Oedipus complex. Dr. Edmund Ziman, in his book *Jealousy in Children,* says that when the young child announces that he is going to marry his mother he is not contemplating incest. All he means is that his mother is the kind of person he likes and that he is secure and happy in her love. The danger comes when a mother has the idea that she has sacrificed herself for her child and is to be repaid by the child's devotion, and so encourages him to love her to the exclusion of everyone else. The mother must wean herself and look for her reward in seeing her child a happy adult.

It seems probable that a great many parents, both fathers and mothers, keep a child playing with them to the exclusion of others just because they themselves enjoy it so much. A questionnaire about what parents and children wished they had more time to do contained eight items.

"Play more with the children" came out third in the parents' replies, but "Play more with my parents" came out eighth (of eight!) in the children's replies. One remedy to the triangle is, therefore, obvious: one of our Onlies remembers, "Mother was always willing to take the *crowd* skating."

Maternal Overprotection

Practically speaking, a parent's love for a child seems to be misguided more often than that of the child for the parent. This is particularly true of a mother's love for her son. It is most particularly true in the child's early years up to adolescence, though the disastrous effects may be evident throughout life. Whenever a mother overprotects a boy she can make life miserable for him. A little Lord Fauntleroy is in a tough spot, even if he is dressed in a space suit.

Levy's *Maternal Overprotection* throws a great deal of light on the symptoms, causes, and results of severe overprotection. It should be stated that Levy picked extreme examples because, as he says, "the study of the maladjusted . . . reveals in sharp relief the points of stress in normal behavior that exclusive study of the normal can never do." Of his twenty cases, nineteen were boys and one a girl. Exactly half of the cases, the girl and nine of the boys, were only children, though the normal expectation would be well under a quarter. This large proportion of Onlies indicates that overprotection is a danger to which parents of an Only should pay special heed.

Extreme maternal overprotection, according to Levy, is most evident in four types of behavior: *excessive contact* (e.g., allowing the child to continue to sleep in the bed with his mother into his teens); *infantilization*, or "babying" (e.g., continuing to dress the child when he is old enough to dress himself); *prevention of independent behavior* (e.g., not allowing the child to walk to school alone when his contemporaries do); and *lack or excess of maternal control* (e.g., letting the child do whatever he wishes or controlling him by an elaborate set of rules).

Levy says that the principal cause of overprotection is "affect hunger," that is, an unsatisfied desire for love. Most of his overprotecting mothers suffered severe privation of parental love in their own childhood, and were presumably trying to satisfy the resultant longing for love. The mothers were generally "responsible, stable, and aggressive" and of a strongly maternal type. Their desire for a child had, in many instances, been long unsatisfied due to difficulties with conception. Frequently they had lost other children at birth or in infancy. Sexual maladjustment in marriage and a lack of outside social contacts were common among these mothers.

The results of overprotection, according to Levy, include disobedience, impudence, and temper tantrums. Though overprotected children who behave in these ways at home generally do well in school (thanks to close association with adults and to parental tutoring), they have marked difficulty in making friends. Many exhibit personality difficulties. When they grow up, they may be poor employment risks.

Our own materials include many cases of obvious overprotection. These show that even when it is not extreme it can have unfortunate results. Two examples follow.

A report from a teacher on one of our Onlies, aged 8 and in Grade III, says: "His mother does everything for him. She drives him to school and opens the car door for him when he arrives there. On cold days she waits for him at the school door and makes sure his coat is buttoned before he ventures out into the cold. Sometimes she comes in and he takes his coat to her and she puts it on him and buttons it. She keeps him home whenever it rains. She also talks baby talk to him. He imitates his mother's gestures, tone of voice, and baby talk. The other children call him 'sugar plum.'

He reads well, but both voice and book shake. He's upset and nervous over failure, and cries." All of which is hard on an 8-year-old boy in Grade III.

One of our 12-year-old Onlies writes: "My major problem centers around my home. I am still babied by my mother. I will admit that I have tried hard to get a tool chest, but in return I'd like to sell my trains. I would like to start a new way of doing things, namely: 1. Not getting my way and acting like the next fellow. 2. Get rid of all traces of babism in me. 3. Be a regular feller. 4. Get a tool chest. 5. And not getting any other thing I want without my own earned money. Also, it has to be useful."

We can see here, perhaps, the genesis of a case which Ziman says is typical, the man bound permanently to a mother whom he hates.

The Dominating Parent

Overprotection may result in indulgence or domination or a mixture of the two. A mother who is concerned about her child's health may be very strict about what he eats and wears, and at the same time coddle him beyond all reason. The form which overprotection takes, Levy says, may be determined by the fundamental temperament of the child. If he is aggressive, he rebels and resists, and his mother (or father) gives in and indulges him. If he is quiet and submissive, he lets his parents continue to exercise control.

That most protecting parents are dominant in the beginning is shown by their insistence on early toilet training. Levy says that seventeen of his twenty overprotected children (including all but one of the Onlies) were dry by the age of 2½ years. (Dr. Benjamin Spock says a fair number of children, especially boys, are not ready to be dry at night before the age of 4.) The Onlies for whom we have information seem to have been trained early and to have had less than the usual number of relapses. One mother says, "The only trouble I ever had with toilet training was not with our son but when we came to housebreaking his dog. And what a time that was for a mother who had been spoiled!" Van Krevelen says that mothers of Onlies toilet-train their children too early and too strictly. He lays this to their abnormal concern with health, and says it continues as an abnormal concern over constipation, the child's and their own. The result, he says, is compulsive cleanliness. Spock blames fights over strict bowel training for "a dread of all kinds of dirtiness," a tendency "to say 'no' to everything," and, in adults, the type of fussy personality that must have everything just so. We have evidence that in recent years, thanks largely to Spock, Gesell, and other writers on child care, battles over bowels are far less frequent than they used to be, even in the case of first or only children.

When the mother plays the dominant role in the family, her son more than probably identifies with her. Then, as Ziman points out, the boy lacks a suitable model for the role he will be supposed to play as a man and a father. If he is not lucky in finding a model outside the family, he may be handicapped for life.

In general, our own cases of dominance seem to include fathers (whom Levy was not studying) as often as mothers. Both father and mother are overstrict in several cases. Our adult Onlies who recall being dominated show resentment and regret when they describe their experiences. One adult, aged 55, says her mother, 80, "is still critical of everything I do and watches my every move when we are together." A young man, 23, says, "My parents have always been very exacting, and closely supervised my development. I've never been able to measure up to their expectations of me, though I have always felt compelled to do what they asked, even though I wasn't interested and knew that it was beyond my ability."

The Only is particularly liable to damage from dominance. When there are two or more children they can support each other against the parents or at least help cover up for each other. Several of our parents of Onlies have said that remembering how their brothers and sisters helped them in the battle of generations has added to their regret at having an Only. The Only is inevitably in the position of meeting every attack single-handed. The force of the dominating parent is concentrated, and the child, being weaker, is almost sure to lose.

The generalized effect on an Only of overprotection, maternal or paternal, indulgent or dominating, is likely to be what van Krevelen calls "fear of development." The Only, he says, is conscious of the help and care he enjoys. Even when he would like to rebel, he is compelled to seek his elders' help. A vicious circle is then set up—he asks, they give. If he meets any trouble he flies back to the nest which his parents are keeping warm. This causes trouble in adjusting to school and in making friends. If the fear of development is not overcome, the only child will continue to hold back in the journey of life. He will lack self-trust and withdraw from every risk. He will always seek a prop. In summing up, van Krevelen quotes the words of a famous Only, John Ruskin, who says that as a child he "disliked growing older—never expected to be wiser, and formed no more plans for the future than a little black silkworm does in the middle of its first mulberry leaf."

IV.

The First Safeguard—Happy Parents

THERE is a saying, "Happy parents make a happy child." And there is another saying, "A happy childhood makes a happy life." Put the two together and you have the reverse of the conditions which we have described in the last two chapters.

Certainly parents who live rich, varied, happy lives of their own have the best chance of maintaining healthy attitudes toward a child and of avoiding such dangers as overprotection.

How the Child Benefits

A child is a little like a passenger in an automobile, who suffers acutely when the driver is overanxious and keeps changing his mind, but is relaxed and cheerful when the driver knows what he is doing and does it without rush or fuss. When parents are secure in their own lives, the child is free from one of the main causes of anxiety. He, too, feels secure.

The child of happy parents enjoys life because he shares directly or vicariously in many of the pleasant things which his parents do.

Good family friends help a child, too. They add to his security because he sees that his parents are accepted in the community. They give him recognition from outside the family and make him feel like somebody in his own right. Their children widen his opportunity to make friends of his own.

And, not least, the child who sees his parents happy in marriage is already learning to be happy in his own marriage when the time comes. He is learning from their example in this as in so many things.

The Happiness Rating of One-Child Marriages

Marriage has been called the great American failure. The American divorce rate is high, and the number of desertions without benefit of divorce enormous. Many couples who present a united front to the world are in reality living in what a serious humorist called "holy deadlock." The emotional suffering involved in these situations is severe for both the partners. The hazards for the mental health and happiness of their children and children's children are even greater. And the burden on an only child is particularly grave.

When the national divorce rate is so high it is not surprising that a large number of couples with only one child do separate. The statistics are, we think, misleading. In 1950, according to reports from sixteen states compiled by the United States Census Bureau, about 23 per cent of all divorces granted were obtained by couples with one child. (More than half the divorces were granted to childless couples.) Of couples with children, 55 per cent had just one child, and the percentage dropped regularly as the number of children increased. Our own statistics show that 8 per cent of our Onlies are children of divorced parents. This is presumably a high percentage, but there are so many variables in the group that no comparison is possible. Our study of Onlies born to Vassar graduates of the classes of 1867-1914 shows that 4 per cent of them are children of divorced parents, while the divorce rate for all Vassar graduates of these classes is 3 per cent. A good many of our Onlies, when asked if they know why they were Onlies, say, "Well, my father and mother didn't get along very well."

The fallacy in the statistics is that divorce does not follow because a couple has one child. Rather, they may have had only one child because they were not well-adjusted in marriage. Too often couples who are not getting on well have a child in a deliberate attempt to save their marriage and then, finding that the child makes matters worse, get divorced. The child is an innocent victim.

If we look at the other side of the picture, at happiness instead of unhappiness in marriage, we find a very different scene. Several investigators have studied happiness in marriage. All agree that, if couples are grouped on the basis of number of children (childless, one child, etc.), the largest percentage of happy marriages is found in the childless group, the next highest percentage is in the group with one child, the next in that with two or three children, and the least in that with four or more children. The Milbank Fund survey of Indianapolis disclosed that 34.8 per cent of the couples with one child rated themselves as happy, against 19.9 per cent with four or more children. Ernest W. Burgess and Leonard Cottrell studied 526 couples, and found that 43.7 per cent with one child were well-adjusted as against 25.5 per cent with two, three, or four children.

Here again one should be cautious about assuming a cause-and-effect relationship. Happily married couples report a desire for children far more than do unhappily married couples. Burgess and Cottrell report that 63.7 per cent of childless couples who still hope for a child have good adjustment as against 20.7 per cent of childless couples who do not wish to have a child. Of couples with one child, 46.8 per cent of those who would like another have good adjustment as against 11.1 per cent of those who do not desire another. In other words, it is the love that inspires a desire for children rather than the number of children which makes for happiness.

Factors in a Happy Marriage

A pretty girl once asked a dramatic critic what she should do to become a good actress. "My dear," he answered, "the first thing is to pick a great actress for a grandmother."

All students of marriage agree that a tradition of happy marriages is one of the surest aids to happy marriage. Lewis Terman, of Stanford University, in his book *Psychological Factors in Marital Happiness,* rated this first and a happy childhood second in the factors conducing to marital happiness. Parents of an only child who want their child to be happy can't go back and live their lives over again. Their view is toward the future. What can they do to make or keep their marriage happy for their child's sake as well as their own?

A statement of Dr. Alfred C. Kinsey's in *Sexual Behavior in the Human Female* is of the utmost importance here. He says, "There seems to be no single factor which is more important for the maintenance of marriage than the determination, the will that that marriage shall be maintained. Where there is that determination, differences between the spouses may be overlooked or forgotten. . . ."

There are thousands of conditions in an infinite variety of combinations which may help make a marriage happy, and, alas, as many that can interfere with happiness. Parents of an only child, if they are already happy, need no advice from marriage counselors or other experts. But the figures on divorce, our own case histories, and studies like Levy's, all indicate that many parents with an only child are not as happy as they might be. Moreover, all of the available information points to three types of difficulty as being especially common in the case histories of parents with maladjusted only children. The three are poor sexual adjustment, a lack of social life as a couple, and a lack of social life as an individual.

Sexual Adjustment

Our case histories do not afford many facts about the sexual adjustment of the parents of our Onlies. Even Kinsey has had difficulty compiling facts about sex. Whatever actual information we have and whatever reasonable deductions we can make give us the impression that parents who are well adjusted sexually are more than likely to have a well-adjusted child, but that unsatisfactory adjustment does not necessarily mean that the child will be maladjusted. There is some indication, however, that where there has been difficulty, the child has had hard work in making a good adjustment. This is certainly true in four cases about which we have details. In two the father became impotent, in another the father contracted a venereal disease, and in the fourth the mother was frigid. But in each case the child has, in the long run, made a good adjustment.

Levy says that satisfactory sexual relations help prevent maternal overprotection. He also says that unsatisfactory sex relations are an accompaniment rather than a cause of maternal overprotection, though they frequently do accompany it. Levy concludes that "the child must bear the brunt of the unsatisfied love life of the mother." In this connection it is notable that cases of concentrated emotion usually involve parent and child of opposite sexes.

Detailed advice on how to improve sex relations is beyond the scope of this book, but because poor sex relations are a frequent cause of Onliness and at least a danger to the only child, some recommendations are in order.

Much sexual maladjustment early in marriage is due to ignorance, but nature usually takes care of this. When, however, the wife continues to fail in achieving an orgasm, there may be increasing tension, fear, and feelings of guilt in both partners. Many parents of only children are particularly vulnerable in this respect, because they marry late and may wonder if they are too old to enjoy the sexual act. Regardless of age, reassurance is the first step to emotional harmony. Couples who find that their own experience is not unusual gain self-respect and confidence and, no longer worried, are quite likely to find themselves immediately achieving what they were trying for in vain before.

Some statements of Kinsey's are of interest here. He says that when people love each other it is not necessary for the wife to have an orgasm either to have pleasure herself or to please her husband. According to his figures, only 63 per cent of women have an orgasm in the first weeks of marriage, and only 75 per cent within the first year. The percentage increases steadily for the *first twenty years*. Maturity, he thinks, is a help in establishing satisfactory sex relations because mature people are less likely than young people to maintain inhibitions.

Determination to make a marriage work is helpful in sex relations as in other aspects of marriage. It will lead the individuals to buy and study books like Dr. Th. H. Van de Velde's *Ideal Marriage* and to be willing to try the techniques which he recommends. If inhibitions remain strong, if intercourse continues to be a trial rather than a pleasure, the determined couple will be willing to talk freely with their doctor and, if he thinks it best, with a psychiatrist or marriage counselor. When one partner feels that the other is unwilling or unhappy in sex relations, the willing partner should take the initiative in seeking advice.

The Parents' Social Life

Someone has pointed out that marriage is the logical way for men and women to satisfy their needs. Shelter, warmth, and the other physical needs, particularly that for food, center around family life. Marriage is the surest way of satisfying the physical drive for reproduction and the emotional needs for love, security, and recognition. And in our contemporary civilization the need for social contacts is, for married couples at least, largely met by a joint social life.

Dr. Hornell Hart calls attention to the fact that the majority of hours which most couples can expect to spend in each other's company coincides with the only times they have free for seeing friends and enjoying recreations. If they do not have or find mutual friends and things they like to do together, they will either go separate ways or, their need for contacts frustrated, become increasingly unpleasant to each other. Levy points out that, in general, a husband depends on his wife for social contacts in the evening. He may feel cheated if his wife is unwilling to make and keep them.

Our case materials show that many parents of only children, even though they are not extremely concentrated on the child or overprotective, nonetheless cramp themselves unreasonably in their social contacts. In a considerable number of these cases, the parents of children 8 to 10 or more years old have never gone out together in the evening. Others go out in the evening and may also take trips, but they always take the child along, despite the fact that he becomes overtired and bored and whines for attention and in general is a nuisance to his parents and their friends.

The usual explanation for a couple's not going out together is that baby sitters are so hard to get. A few parents cite horrific examples of baby sitters who got drunk or went home early or turned out to be perverts, and say they are not willing to take the risk. Such disasters do happen. The fact remains that millions and millions of parents, including a fair share of those with only children, do leave children with baby sitters more frequently than for an occasional evening and, if they are going on a trip, arrange for a housekeeper to take charge of the child in their absence. Furthermore, many only children of 9 or 10 or so are perfectly capable of spending an hour or two alone (see Chapter XI, "When Should Your Child Stay Alone?").

Parents with a desire to watch over their child every minute find excuses easily. One couple who had gone off for a short trip, leaving the grandparents in charge, came home to find that their son had hunted up his woolly panda and was taking it to bed with him. This, they decided, was a sign that the child was emotionally upset by their absence, so on their next trip they took the child along. Of course the child may have been upset, but there was no sign that he was seriously disturbed. The panda may very well have been all the comfort he needed. And it is more than probable that, having had the experience of his parents' being away and returning with gifts for him, he would actually have welcomed their absence next time.

A mother who asked us how much she should leave her child alone never gave us a chance to answer. Instead she began quoting various authorities, ourselves included (!), to the effect that parents see much too little of their children and do too few things with them. She was already planning not to send her son to camp or away to school or college because "We are a lot older and he may not have us very long."

Some parents just can't face leaving their child out of the fun. They may laugh and call him "little Me Too" but they succumb to his pleas to be taken along. Grace Langdon and Irving W. Stout, in their book *The Discipline of Well-Adjusted Children,* emphasize the need of give-and-take for happy family relations. The only child has a special need to learn to give, and Langdon and Stout cite the case of a well-adjusted Only who wanted to ride to town with his parents: "'Can I go?' The father replied, 'Nope, this is Ma's and my night to bowl, Bud. You can go next time.' To which the boy replied, 'Aw shucks, but all right.'"

A couple who feel that they are tying themselves too close to their child have several means of cutting the knots or at least giving themselves—and the child—more rope.

A good way to start is by entertaining more. Ask other couples in for a card game or a drink or a meal or all three. Some people find it easier to do this if they set aside a definite evening each week for entertaining. Try to invite different couples so that your circle of friends—and, potentially, your child's—expands. Don't excuse yourselves by saying, "But they've never asked us." Formality of this sort would freeze any community. Make a point of finding out what your guests do about baby sitters; there are almost always a few in each neighborhood who are known to be reliable. When you are invited out in return, get a baby sitter and go.

Couples clubs are an easy way to social contacts. Many churches have such clubs, and almost every school has a parents' association. There's quite likely to be a newcomers' club in town, too. One way to meet people in any town is to join a church and to take part in its activities.

The emphasis which we have placed on contacts with other people does not mean that we rule out amusements to be enjoyed by the couple alone. Pleasures shared in private are fun and they add strength to a marriage. Couples should surely arrange to have time by themselves to go to the movies, to dine out, to play tennis, and to take trips.

Travel without the child is hard to arrange but most beneficial. Change and freedom from routine and responsibility are the essence of a vacation. Our materials show several arrangements that allow parents of only children to go away. One couple has a reciprocal agreement with neighbors and, when either is away for a night or more, the children visit the other. Grandparents and other relatives are an invaluable resource. A fortunate few have servants or are able to employ a temporary housekeeper. Some wait until the child is in camp. All of these arrangements afford good experience in independence for the child, and there is no better way for parents to wean themselves than to take a trip away from home without their child.

Separate Activities

Husbands and wives profit from vacations from each other, too. A wise wife, who happens to be one of our Onlies, said, "If a husband doesn't see a lot of other people he doesn't know how good his wife is to him." And an only child who is left sometimes with one parent and sometimes with the other benefits in many ways. He learns to know the parent he is with better. This sounds strange, but many children are in the position of the Only who said, "I loved my father but I never really knew him. He never did anything with me." The child who sometimes has each parent to himself feels more secure, because he feels that each parent is interested in him and willing to pay attention to him and take care of him. When the parent in question is of the same sex, the child has the opportunity for, and an added stimulus to, identification. When the parent is of the opposite sex, the child plays the role of an adult partner.

A mother, who spent her first night away from her only child when the girl was 11, was very nervous. She kept imagining all the things that could go wrong. When she got back home the next night she found that both husband and daughter had had a beautiful time. The girl had proved to herself that she was capable of managing a home.

In general, husbands have more outside contacts than do wives. They go to work in the daytime, and after working hours have chances to associate with fellow employees. If wives had more duties that took them out of the house and

more automatic social contacts, there would be less maternal overprotection. As it is, most wives must strive for some
independent social life. It's up to their husbands to give
them moral and practical encouragement. Not the least
thing the husband can do is to volunteer to baby-sit regularly on the night the Mothers Club meets. He ought, too,
to urge his wife to leave the child with him or with a paid
baby sitter and do things like playing cards with a group
of friends, attending a hobby-club meeting or exhibition,
going off to a college reunion, shopping in the city, or just
going to the movies. The opportunities are endless, provided
the husband will cooperate and the wife will realize that
she is more than justified, that she is actually promoting
family happiness, if she occasionally breaks away.

Mothers often say that they can't make time for social
activities. The mother with only one child is in a strategic
position here because she has relatively less to do in the
way of family chores. One plan for regular contacts de-
serves wider trial. A group of mothers of school-age children in a suburban community see their husbands off on
an early train, drop their children at school, and, once a
week, gather at 8:45 A.M. to play bridge. They are the scan-
dal of the neighborhood, but we think they're smart.

Fun with the Family

The happiest one-child families that we know manage to
make time for the husband and wife to have social contacts
as a couple, for each to maintain separate interests and hobbies, and for parents and child to share activities together.

Of course, most families do share many hours of company.
More often than not they are together the first thing in the
morning, and again from late afternoon until the child's
bedtime. A little thought and effort, particularly by the father, can make these shining hours.

These are the hours that afford the child a chance to

learn from the example of his parents. Of course, deliberately setting a good example every minute might make even an Army sergeant a self-conscious prig, and parents who are prigs will have a priggish child. It isn't necessary to be something you are not. But you should show friendly interest in what other members of the family are doing and lend a helping hand when you can. If you are the father you should be particularly careful not to draw into your shell like an old turtle whenever you are at home. Don't be like the father whose child drew his portrait as a pair of hands holding up a newspaper.

If a mother and father still *converse* with each other at meal times, if they exchange ideas, make jokes, and argue out differences of opinion, a child learns from them how to talk and to talk well. There is a danger, of course, that he will hear "overmuch adult conversation" and begin to talk about matters that are way beyond his years or experience. Therefore, when the child is present, parents should refrain as far as they can from gossip and from discussing problems that the child might not understand or that might worry him. The child profits most if the conversation is intrinsically interesting to him and concerns something about which he can have and express a valid opinion.

When a child is too young to come to the table for every meal—and there's a temptation to have an only child begin eating with the family too soon—he may well be invited as a special treat regularly once or twice a week. These meals can be made something of a party. One mother always marks the Friday night family supper by doing eggs in a chafing dish at the table. As a child grows older the special night may remain a sort of party night, even though the child is now attending all meals.

Bossard, who advocates regular family parties complete with good china, etiquette, and after-dinner talk, points out a danger in the one-child family's celebration of recurring festivals. The parents, pleased, for example, by a child's cuteness over his first Christmas stocking and unconsciously desiring to keep him a baby dependent on them, may repeat a ritual on a babyish level just to prevent the child's growing up and away from them. The remedy is to invite other children of the same age to share the fun. The parents probably won't baby their child in front of his friends, but, if they do, the friends will soon set him straight.

There is, too, a danger in the other direction. An only child, constantly exposed to adult conversation and manners, may become too old for his years. Lots of association with other children is one remedy for this. The safeguard within the family circle is to plan *joint activities* at the child's level. A father can enjoy playing trains with his 7-year-old son much more than that son can enjoy practicing putting with his father. In fact, the child's sex and level of interest should always be considered in the choice of games. Parents who have any question about what might interest a boy or girl of a given age should consult the "play gradient" in *The Child from Five to Ten*, by Gesell and Ilg, and the chapter "Fun with the Family" in our *Better Home Discipline*.

Another wise precaution is to plan for the child to do things now with one parent, now with another, and sometimes with both. This scheme protects against division of the family into two camps and also gives each parent some time to himself.

When Both Parents Work

Both parents of an only child often work. This is true regardless of social level. We have cases where the parents are factory workers and where they are professional people.

"Should mothers work?" is a very controversial question. Mothers, both those who work and those who don't, feel very strongly about the matter and not always on the side one would expect. Some think the mother's added interest and the extra money contribute to family happiness. Others think that a mother is justified in working only in case of dire need. Experts are divided in their opinions. We see a good many advantages on the side of working, particularly for the mother of an only child, but our case materials also disclose some dangers and the need for certain precautions.

The reasons for the mother of an only child working are not far to seek, expecially if the child is in school and her husband is employed all day. She has, compared with the mothers of several children, relatively little to do in the way of housework. Her house or apartment may be small and well-equipped with labor-saving devices. There is no younger child to keep her at home. She is lonely and perhaps bored. Moreover she is probably ambitious for her child and hopes that by working she can add to family savings to be used to send him to school and college and help him get started in the world.

There is an advantage for a mother of an only child in work which takes her out of the home. Her employment gives her the kind of contact that men have and serves as a safeguard, though not a guaranty, against overprotection. Moreover, the work itself, or at least the gossip of the firm, gives the mother a live interest outside her family. She benefits, and, because she has extra interests, so does her child. If the mother's work is with the father or in line with his work, there is another common interest to bind the marriage.

The disadvantages stem from the danger that the child's needs will go unsatisfied. The very young child needs the love and loving care that a good mother supplies better than any nurse or relative. The somewhat older child, the one who is in his early years at school, certainly profits from having someone to come home to, especially if he stays all day at school and has his lunch there. He may dawdle home, or stop en route to play football (tearing his best pants) and not reach home until his mother is starting to prepare supper. Even so, the fact that she is there adds to his security. And if something has happened during the day that is particularly exciting or worrying he needs the chance to burst out and tell her about it.

We feel, then, that the mother of a preschool child ought to make her child her job if she doesn't absolutely have to work to support the family. We feel that, at least until the child is 10, a mother with a child in school ought to try to arrange her work to be home when he comes home, both at lunchtime, if he comes home to lunch, and in the afternoon. Here are some of our reports on only children both of whose parents work, apparently to the detriment of the child.

A boy in second grade had been cantankerous about dressing one morning, when his mother was hurrying to get off to her job. He had been scolded and told he would be punished. He came home from school in the afternoon and got the house key from the neighbor next door. His mother came home to find him sitting in a corner facing the wall, punishing himself because he had been slow in the morning. That seems to us a bad way for a 7-year-old boy to spend a sunny afternoon.

Another, a 9-year-old girl, has pretty brown curls and a sweet personality but a bad complexion. The teacher asked the school doctor to examine the child. He reported, "She's dirty. All she needs is a thorough washing every day."

A 7-year-old boy goes to a neighbor's for lunch and back to the neighbor's after school. There he helps scrub floors, wash dishes, and do other housework until he is picked up just before supper. A teacher, who asked him if there were any children in his neighborhood with whom he liked to play, says he "first looked puzzled and then shook his head."

A high-school senior with a good IQ had very poor marks. Investigation disclosed that for some years he had been working after school, in the evenings, and on Saturdays—any time he could get a job. There was no shortage of money—both parents had good salaries. The boy was just imitating the example of his parents and, like his parents, enjoying the good things money can buy. He is of college caliber but hasn't grades high enough to get in.

There is a possibility that some mothers work in preference to caring for a child because they are unconsciously rejecting the child. Work and the extra money are then excuses for getting away, for strict control with a view to keeping the child from interfering, and even for neglect. When a husband suspects this may be the case, when he knows the extra money is not needed and the child seems to be on the short end of the deal, he must take the initiative in correcting it. Arguments and recriminations will be worse than useless. Professional help is needed. The first step is to put the facts before the family doctor.

In general, however, the working mother has reason on her side. She and the child have much to gain, and thoughtful planning can obviate many of the difficulties. The best planning requires more than a consideration of the age of the child and the mother's hours of work. Vacations, what fun the mother and child can share without overtiring the mother, and how to check on the child's adjustment and progress seem the most important items. As the child grows older his cooperation in planning and in checking his own progress is essential. He needs to understand that his mother's work is important to her, either as a career or economically or both, but is not a denial of him. He should be encouraged to do his part in promoting the happiness of the family.

V.

Discipline vs. Spoiling

SEVENTY years ago a young woman, accompanied by a 4-year-old boy, was waiting to take a train. Her small charge went scampering up and down the platform reading the advertising posters that even in those days adorned stations and helped impatient travelers pass the time.

A sour, gray-haired woman approached our heroine and snapped: "That child is too young to be reading!"

"Is he? I hadn't thought."

"And how old are you?"

"Twenty-three."

"And he's an only child, I presume."

"On the contrary, the youngest of six!"

The sour one departed, snorting her disbelief, and the 23-year-old called to her youngest brother.

This story of the past shows that the popular idea that the only child is allowed to do whatever he wants without interference from his parents is an old one. And our case histories show that, though few Onlies seem spoiled badly if at all, spoiling is still a matter of great concern to parents of Onlies and to Onlies themselves.

What Parents and Onlies Say about Spoiling

A typical attitude is that of the mother who wrote: "Our son, aged 6, is an only child and so, while we have tried very hard not to spoil him, we have also had more time and attention available for him than we would have had were there more children, and have been able to teach him much through reasoning and example. He received what is, I presume, the average amount of spankings when he was little, and so he learned quickly and thoroughly the meaning of 'No.' Now, although he is not perfect by any means, he is, as we both want him to be, a regular boy with at least average intelligence and an excellent memory. We can almost always correct him by talking. I cannot remember when the last time was that he required more severe punishment, or for what. Children grow so quickly out of one phase and into another. Perhaps we have more drastic times ahead of us. We'll have to wait and see."

One woman, now in her fifties, says: "I was constantly being given things beyond my family's means—private school, boarding school, a big debut party, Pullman tickets. And they let me quit college after a year just because I didn't like it. So I was very strict with my first child. He fought back and is still belligerent and aggressive."

A man in his forties reports: "I had everything my own way. When I was in my teens, my father died. My mother tried to control me, but I still did whatever I wanted despite the friction. It was hard on me when I went into the Army and had to learn to get on with others and to do what I was told. But the Army helped me learn so that now I get on pretty well in the office and in my marriage."

Not all of our reports admit that Onlies might be spoiled. In fact, some Onlies are quite indignant about their reputation. A 15-year-old girl writes, "My major problem at home is getting blamed for everything since I am the only child. I am the only one who can take the blame." And one of our adult Onlies says, "There was no chance of my being spoiled—there were three adults to jump on me whatever I did."

The Spoiled Adult

Most of our adult Onlies show no signs of being spoiled. Even those who say they were spoiled as children have outgrown the ill effects, sometimes to the surprise of their acquaintances. One teacher, speaking of an Only whom she had taught many years ago, says, "He was rather spoiled, but he's very agreeable now."

Spoiling can, however, have a continuing bad effect. A study of Onlies serving prison terms for second offenses states that they blame their lot on having been spoiled as children. We have no first-hand histories of prison inmates, but we've seen adult Onlies who behaved like spoiled children. For example, one young man was invited to play tennis doubles as the partner of his new employer. Whenever a ball was knocked out of court and had to be chased, the young man would let the older man do it. He behaved the same way on his job. He expected other people to do the dull, unpleasant things and to wait on him. He lost the job.

One woman says, "I can always have what I want if I am careful to lead my husband around by the nose." Of another woman, whose father spoiled her badly, a friend says, "Now she's married and she has just what she wants. She wheedles around until she gets it."

We have several cases of Onlies who have made poor records in college, marriage, employment, or all three because they continued to behave like spoiled children. There are enough such cases to serve as a warning; countermeasures are definitely in order.

The Antidote: Better Home Discipline

In our book *Better Home Discipline,* we wrote: "The spoiled child is a 'grabber' long after he should have learned to share and to wait. He doesn't control his impulses, and so misses a lot of advantages that he would have if he could learn to wait and to work for what he wants." The remedy which we proposed was firm and consistent parental control. We felt, and feel, that it is far better for a child to be well disciplined at home than to have to learn by being criticized and perhaps ostracized in school. Other psychologists have found that firm and consistent discipline in childhood is favorable to good adjustment in the teens, strong initiative, mental health, and marital happiness.

A child who has siblings is more subject to control than is an Only. In the large family everyone has to learn to keep out of the way, to take turns, to wait, and in general not to interfere with others. If the parents do not control a child, his siblings will, perhaps harshly. Parents of an Only have to serve as parents and siblings, too. They do not need to be harsh, but they do have to be determined. One of our best-adjusted Onlies, the child of well-to-do parents, says: "My mother was determined I wouldn't be spoiled. One of her plans was always to make me wait for the proper time before I got something. I couldn't eat before meals. When I wanted a bike I had to wait for my birthday, and not use it the day before, either."

A Good Start

The right way to behave, like any other accomplishment, is better learned by doing right than by doing wrong and being corrected. You can help a child establish a habit of behaving well if you will cultivate skill in giving directions. Here are some pointers from the experience of generations of parents:

Be sure you have the child's attention.

Use a pleasant tone of voice. There's rarely any need to speak sharply, and a harsh tone gets a child's back up.

Give advance notice of an impending order. This sets the child's mind to obey when the minute comes.

Establish routines. A child who always goes to bed at eight makes less fuss than one who goes sometimes at seven-forty-five and sometimes at eight-fifteen.

Give directions positively. This avoids the chance of the child's refusing a request like "Will you——." Suggesting a substitute for poor behavior is more effective than a plain "Stop that."

A Minimum of Rules Consistently Enforced

Rules, like routines, help a child know what to do in given circumstances, instill in him good habits, and increase his security, *if they are wise rules consistently enforced.* The cardinal principle of rules is to keep them to the minimum necessary for the child's safety and the family's convenience. The smaller the number of rules, the more likely you and the child are to remember them. It is foolish to make a rule that you do not enforce consistently. A rule broken with impunity is worse than a rule never made, because the child thinks, when next he is tempted, "Well, I'll probably get away with it." And if he does get away with it often enough, he may carry this attitude through life and be a spoiled adult.

Another great advantage in keeping rules to a minimum is that the child has more opportunities to discipline himself. He learns self-control when he finds out for himself what things are good to do and what not to do. Of course you don't let a child do anything which you can see will hurt him seriously. But the more you can refrain from scolding and from a stream of nagging "Don'ts," the better. Try asking yourself, "Does it really matter?" "Will he outgrow it?" and "Is it bothering anybody?"

Praise

Praise has been called "the magic wand of discipline." Parents who praise what they sincerely like, and, whenever possible, ignore what they disapprove, work miracle after miracle. The child's need for recognition is best satisfied by his parents' approval. When he realizes how he can gain that approval he will work and work for it. Praise that is really earned results in the reverse of spoiling. It teaches the child to restrain his impulses while he strives to reach a distant goal, and it heads him toward unselfish goals which win the approval of others.

There are, however, dangers in praise. Too much praise too easily given teaches a child to be satisfied with, and conceited about, trivial achievements, half-hearted efforts, and good intentions. He is not taught the satisfaction of hard persistent work. And when parents praise a child for obeying orders but hold back praise, even scold, when a child shows initiative, there is no stimulus to self-discipline and responsibility.

Reasoning

Reason, like praise, can be a powerful instrument of good discipline but inflict sharp wounds when used by over-indulgent or dominating parents. The overindulgent spoil the young child by accepting a ceaseless stream of "Why? Why? Why?" as evidence of reason when all the child is doing is distracting the parent from an intended correction. As the child grows older he becomes prolific with excuses and alibis, and the indulgent parent who accepts these as reasons teaches the child to shirk duties. The dominating parent who sets out to use reason may too often end up by scolding or at least doing all the talking himself. He believes he is reasonable and reasoning, but true reason is a matter of give-and-take.

The good parent learns to listen more than he talks. Most children, like most adults, who are given a chance to talk out their troubles and to discuss their plans soon convince themselves of where they have gone, or may go, wrong. For example, a child who offers feeble excuses or alibis recognizes their feebleness as he hears himself voice them. The parent does not need to argue with him or to be sarcastic. A grin is enough to restore the child to the right track.

Occasionally the good listener has to put in a word to keep the child talking. If the child is angry or upset, the parent can help him release feelings by saying, "I know, you're mad at me. I used to get mad at my parents, too," or, "I know just how you feel. That same thing once happened to me." If a child is really puzzled, and if he is used to talking with his parents, he will ask for advice. When he does, he is ready to act upon it. Give it to him as simply as possible and leave as many of the details as possible for him to work out for himself.

The parents of an only child usually have the time to talk with him, to let him say what he wishes to do and why. In case of need, they can take time to explain why he should not do something. If the parents are clever they can help a child to learn to think straight. There are some precautions which must be exercised. When a parent gives a direct order he should expect instant obedience; a child who stops to argue might be run over. A child should not be allowed to talk himself out of situations when he has misbehaved deliberately and knows he should be punished. The parent should be on his guard against letting the child distract him from the main issue.

The Family Council

The best use of reasoning and the best training in reasoning both come when reasoning is used as a part of planning constructively. And the best opportunity for planning is afforded by a family council.

Some parents to whom we've suggested a family council have thought that their family was too small for such a formal procedure. If they have read *Cheaper by the Dozen*,

with its enthusiastic account of the Gilbreth council, they
are quite likely to say that a tribal council is fine but a
three-member committee rather pointless. We think they are
mistaken in the latter opinion.

The council in a small family need not be formal but it
should meet regularly. Sunday after breakfast, if the family
has the pleasant habit of lingering over the table then, is a
good time. All that is necessary is to have the father or
mother say, "Well, what's coming up this week?" If each
parent talks briefly about plans, the child will, too. A family
goal—a trip to be planned, a boat to be painted, a house to
be built—is a natural topic for discussion. A child of 8 or 9
can take part if the parents are careful to steer clear of
problems that might worry him unduly. The more constructive the topics, the better. If a child's mistakes come up, as
they probably will, they can be dealt with reasonably. The
most important thing to remember is that a council is a
council and not a session of the grand jury. It follows that
each member has a right to express his own opinion and
to listen to what the others say. If everyone is free to talk,
the group will reach agreement. There may and should be
compromises, but all will be ready to give the decision a
fair trial. An only child who regularly has this experience
learns to think for himself, to express himself, to respect
others, and to cooperate. And, because he feels sure of family backing, he feels proud and secure.

The Use and Abuse of Punishment

Ideally, no punishment is necessary to support good discipline. Most children, if they know what their parents
expect of them and if their parents do not expect too much,
try hard to conform. Only children, because they gain most
of their recognition from their parents, are overwhelmingly
anxious not to do anything to cause parental disapproval.
But, in practice, a child's urge for independence occasion-

ally brings him into conflict with adult ideas of safety, manners, and order. Then he has to learn that behavior which endangers himself or others and behavior which transgresses the rights of others have unpleasant consequences.

A child had better learn from his parents, through punishment if necessary, that he must not run out into traffic than learn his lesson by being hit by a car. He had better learn to respect others' property, including his parents', by being punished when he misappropriates something at home than find out in school how unpopular such behavior makes him with other children. Parents of Onlies have to be on the alert to notice and disapprove behavior which they might indulge as cute but which other children might punish by fighting or, worse, ostracism. Here the parents must put themselves in the place of brother and sister and be as strict and uncompromising as brothers and sisters are. If the child continues to behave in a way that might interfere with his making friends, his parents will have to punish him for it.

The immediate purpose of punishment is to prevent repetition of misbehavior. The long-range goal is to help the child learn not to behave in ways that might damage his good social relations with other people, including his parents.

The danger in punishment is that it will damage a child emotionally, by convincing him that he is not loved, by stirring profound resentment, or by causing him to suppress feelings that will then find vent in some other and perhaps more difficult behavior. Because most punishment is administered when both child and parent are upset, parents do well to set their minds ahead of time to follow a few definite principles:

Be prompt. Promptness helps the child associate punishment and crime and remember the possible consequences next time he is tempted to behave in the same way.

Make the punishment fit the crime. This, too, aids memory. It helps the child see that misbehavior has unpleasant results. And it makes the punishment seem fair to him.

Be brief. Prolonged punishment estranges the child. The briefest, simplest, easiest punishment that works is the best.

Let bygones be bygones. Once the child has been punished, take the first opportunity to reassure him of your love and liking. Then he realizes that you were punishing the deed and not him.

Be consistent. If you punish a given type of misbehavior one day and not the next, you just teach the child to take a chance. If he knows that retribution follows transgression as night the day, he will learn to control his impulses. Every time he resists temptation he is pleased, because he knows he is avoiding punishment, and this pleasure reinforces his desire to behave well.

The Question of Spanking

To many people punishment unfortunately means spanking. There's more than a suspicion in our minds that the popular comment on a spoiled child, "He needs a good spanking," has caused a lot of unnecessary suffering for only children and their mothers. There are worse punishments than spanking, but there are also better. We have no criticism to make of mothers who spank young children, if both child and mother take it in a matter-of-fact manner. When spanking is the custom of the neighborhood a child may even think it *comme il faut.* One mother remembers how she got mad at her 10-year-old Only and sent him upstairs. She followed and rather inexpertly whacked him across the buttocks. He grinned and said, "Why, Mother, are you *spanking* me? Like Jack's mother?"

But we see no point in spanking if the mother suffers or the Only has a strong emotional reaction. The mother of one Only, aged 8 years, says, "When Phyllis does something she shouldn't I spank her. I turn her face down across my lap so she can't see *my* tears. I hate doing it, but I'll not raise a spoiled brat."

What Other Parents Find Best

Years of questioning parents and children about methods of punishment leave us with no doubt that *depriving a child of a possession or privilege* is both the most-used and the most-effective punishment. Depriving often has the merit of fitting the crime. A child who rides his bike in the street against orders is deprived of his bike for a week. Taking away any privilege usually produces results. A mother writes: "I have a big problem with my son, aged 12. Being an only child he has been spoiled a great deal. I find at times he wants his own way, but this is soon rectified by taking away the privilege of staying up until nine on school nights. Believe me, this hurts, because he does enjoy watching TV."

Isolating a child from a playmate or a situation that is making him misbehave is another favorite method. It has the merit of removing him from the cause of the trouble. If he is allowed to return as soon as he thinks he can behave, he may learn that a determination to exercise self-control is a source of strength. But if he weakens quickly, he should be isolated again and for a definite time.

Making right as far as he can any damage he has done is a good lesson in responsibility for a child. This is a favorite measure when a child has accidentally broken or spilled something. Parents do well to remember that a child is usually as sorry as they are when he drops a glass of milk. Cleaning it up helps him work off his emotion, and at the same time teaches him that carelessness makes work.

Scolding and additional punishments aren't necessary. In fact, it's a good idea for the parents to pitch in and help with the job, provided they let the child do all he can. Their help will show him that he is forgiven and make him try more than ever not to have the same kind of accident again.

Find the Cause

If you can find out why a child is misbehaving you are in a strategic position to help him. Any misbehavior may be due to fatigue or hunger or some developing illness. Chronic misbehavior may be due to chronic illness or to some unsatisfied emotional need. If a child feels he is not loved, or if he feels insecure, or if he is not getting recognition for things he does right, he will misbehave just to force his parents to pay attention to him.

When an Only is consistently defiant and impertinent—when, for example, he regularly refuses to go to bed when he is told, to come in when called, to stop play, to wash, or to come to meals—there is more than a chance that he is being consistently overindulged. One of the paradoxes of indulgent overprotection is that the mother will complain bitterly about the way a child defies her and in the same breath offer alibis for him: "I can't make him come when I call him, and of course, being an Only, he does need all the play with other children he can have."

Alibis offered by the parent are almost a sure sign of overindulgence. So is the unwillingness of a child to obey a parent though he regularly obeys teachers or baby sitters: "He's quite a handful at home but OK in school."

Overindulgent parents, mothers or fathers, will not find changing their own attitudes an easy matter. When indulgence is not just habit but a means of satisfying some deepseated personal need of the parent's, change is particularly difficult. There are, in any case, some ways to help oneself change. It is wise to remember the dangers in indulgence and to determine to control the act even when the desire is present. An attempt to stop one or two specific forms of indulgence is more likely to be successful than an attempt at a general change. If you can first gain a child's respect in a particular matter, you will find him more ready to cooperate in other matters later. Limit the orders which you give to those you are determined to enforce; don't, for example, call a child from play if you can excuse his not coming. Make up your mind how you will punish him if he disobeys an order or a rule, and carry out your intention. Do not make threats. A threat is often impossible to fulfill, and failure to carry out a threat, like failure to punish a child who breaks a rule, teaches the child to take a chance.

Overindulgent parents who are able to change will find great rewards. Their own convenience is not the least of these. The greatest is the increased happiness of the child. The spoiled child is an unhappy child. The child who respects his parents' authority has a sense of security that lets him enjoy life.

Teamwork

One of the great sources of inconsistency is lack of teamwork between parents. Even a husband and wife who love, like, and respect each other can unconsciously strive for the favors of an only child. When parents are not happily married, when there is any tension between the parents, when they are sexually maladjusted, or when they have little outside social life together, they can become outright rivals for the child's affection. Each needs love, and the child is the source most readily available. A baby of 2 can and will take advantage of a situation like this, and older children may use it to avoid all duties and responsibilities. They get a double dose of spoiling. A study by Martha Lewenberg of the factors causing maternal overprotection discloses a very high proportion of cases in families where social maladjustment, sexual maladjustment, and disagreement over discipline are all three present.

An Only who is the father of an Only writes: "I became so disgusted at the ease with which I could play one parent against the other that in our own marriage we reached early agreement that no instruction to the children (this was before we knew that our Only would be an Only) would be questioned in the slightest by the other parent. This is possibly the one theory of which we have made a 100 per cent practice. It has had an amusing outgrowth, in that both parents, realizing that an order, once stated, would be inflexible, whichever issued it, began to seek counsel beforehand. At about the age of 10, our son began to participate, and the committee system, at least for us, works."

An Only married to an Only and now the mother of two happy children writes: "Parents should strive to be in accord with each other on all matters pertaining to the discipline of an only child. In that way the Only will not try to play them against each other and will love them equally, *which increases his feeling of security*." We have italicized the last clause because we agree so heartily.

The Father's Part

Many parents who disagree over discipline are far from maladjusted in their marriage. The disagreement can, nonetheless, have serious consequences. The usual pattern is for the father to take less and less part in bringing up the child. This is particularly hard on a boy, because it makes it difficult for him to identify with his father and to learn to play a man's role.

Mothers inevitably bear the major responsibility for discipline. This is as it should be. The mother is home more than the father and so is in charge when a child does things which need correcting. If she says, "Wait till I tell your father," she is making three mistakes: she is failing to act promptly; she is subjecting the child to prolonged worry; she is making him fear his father. And, if the father doesn't support her, she's encouraging the child to misbehave when she is in charge. Firmness and consistency demand that when the mother is in charge she take whatever action is necessary and, if the child appeals to the father, that the father back her up.

All of this sounds more terrible than it usually is in practice. If the mother is firm and consistent, troubles are infrequent, and there is almost never anything sufficiently important for either child or mother to remember long enough to take up with the father. But if the father has any reason to believe that all is not well, he should check himself very carefully to be sure that he is fulfilling all his duties as a parent.

A kindergarten teacher reported: "I have a 5-year-old boy who is incorrigibly disobedient. He hits other children, causes trouble, and obeys no one. He is an only child and a spoiled child. His father has spoiled him; his mother is nervous and rather frail. She can't and does not control him for the most part; occasionally she threatens him with physical punishment. As a result, he scoffs at good behavior and does as he pleases. He does not take commands seriously; he merely smiles and disobeys." We suggested that the teacher visit the home. She later reported: "I talked with the father, who, it seemed to me, had done most of the harm by condoning all the bad actions of the boy as merely 'naughty.' I impressed the father with the fact that his son needed more discipline and that he was the only one who could do it satisfactorily. The problem was settled by the father's cooperation. The father has a good deal of influence with the boy and persuaded him to listen and to obey others as well as the father. The plan has succeeded rather well."

Levy, in talking of the treatment in his twenty cases of maternal overprotection, describes several where improved relationships between father and child helped greatly. The sons developed friendlier feelings and increased respect for their fathers and so were aided "in overcoming dependencies on the mother through an increasing identification with the father in adolescence and young manhood."

Dr. William Griffiths of the University of Minnesota has studied what children think their parents expect of them. He concludes, "The father represents primarily a person not to be interfered with," because he principally wants the child not to interrupt him and to be less noisy. If you are a father and share these feelings, you may take comfort from the fact that they are not unusual. But you will still wish to do something to change matters and help your child. We suggest:

Spend some time alone with the child each week.

Do things with the child that the child likes. A child doesn't always enjoy weeding just because his father likes to garden, nor yet helping his father polish the car. He does usually enjoy going for a ride, especially if he can take a young friend along, and any kind of sport from passing a football to fishing. But if he doesn't want to be interrupted in what he is doing, don't insist.

Take your child to visit the place where you work. Your colleagues will be nice to the child and to you. You will become more of a person in your child's eyes, and, if he is a boy, he will find you a more definite model.

Give your wife at least one night a week off by taking full charge of the child and house while she visits friends or goes to the movies.

Don't pass the buck to your wife. When you're in charge, take command. It's even worse for a father to say, "We'll ask your mother," than for a mother to say, "Wait till I tell

Daddy." But try not to encourage behavior you know your wife doesn't like. Fathers as well as mothers can overindulge and overprotect children.

Read "Fathers Are Parents, Too," by Dr. O. Spurgeon English. You'll find lots of food for thought and many practical suggestions.

VI.

Some Common Behavioral and Emotional Problems of Young Onlies

SOME problems are specially deserving of study when they occur in an only child. Other children behave in these same ways, but there is a chance in the case of an Only that the cause may be one of the particular hazards of Onliness. There are also some kinds of misbehavior which are so in line with the popular idea of the shortcomings of an Only that the parents will want to be sure both to correct them and to use them as an object lesson in teaching the child what an Only should not do.

Feeding Problems

Some investigators have found that refusal to eat and food fads are somewhat more common in Onlies than in children in general. Our case histories of only children show that a considerable number may be expected to present feeding problems. We find cases of Onlies who refuse to eat, eat desserts but nothing else, overeat of things they like, and eat between meals. We have a few cases of obesity in adult Onlies, who are certainly not helped by habits of self-indulgence in eating.

Of course, problems connected with feeding are common in all sizes of families. An Only who won't eat, or wants to subsist on candy, has plenty of company. But his mother must ask herself if she is either overindulgent or overstrict. If she is either of these in the matter of feeding, she may be so in other matters, too. A feeding problem may be a clue to the need for a broad change in methods of discipline.

What happens when a mother indulges her child's food fads is shown by the case of Virginia. Virginia, aged 7 years, is a finicky eater and suffers from indigestion and from an allergy to cottonseed oil. Cottonseed oil is commonly used in the preparation of potato chips, and this child and her parents are inordinately fond of them. There's usually a bag on the kitchen shelf. Virginia will refuse to eat her lunch. An hour or so later she will beg for "just one chip." Her mother, and her father if he is at home, will say, "Just one." More begging, more "Just one" answers. One plus one plus one, etc., soon means a whole bag of chips, a stomach ache, and a rash. At supper time Virginia has no appetite and refuses the milk and juice and other foods which the doctor thinks she should have.

A teen-age girl who was similarly indulged as a child is now too fat. She makes a great show of dieting and regularly refuses dessert at the table. A few minutes later she very quietly reaches out and helps herself. Still later she goes to the kitchen, takes the leftover dessert from the refrigerator, and "cleans it up."

The Only who, because of overindulgence or temperamental lack of self-control, cannot control an appetite for sweets has no brothers and sisters to tease her (or him!) out of it. Brothers and sisters have a way of being aware of each other's weaknesses and they are merciless in exposing them. Parents cannot bring themselves to be so cruel. They can, and should, check their own impulses to allow "just one" and "just one more." They can, if potato chips are bad for a child and the parents know they can't be firm, keep chips out of the house.

A child who refuses to eat certain foods or is inclined to overindulge in a given food can be helped if his parents will occasionally invite some of his young friends to meals. It's probable that they will be on their good behavior and eat everything. The small host, wanting to conform, will follow their good example. The experience may even teach him that foods which he has been refusing are good. And, because he is on his good behavior or because he fears teasing, he won't dive into one dish. But we won't guarantee that he and his friends wouldn't clean up a bag of chips if they happened on it just before lunch.

A mother who suspects that she is overindulgent does well to think back over the history of the child's weaning. The typically overprotective mother is very slow to wean her baby from breast or bottle. If the baby shows any reluctance to take food from a spoon or cup, she tells herself, despite what her doctor and her baby bible say, that the baby is not ready to change, or that he needs strength, or that fondling is good for a child. Running counter to the pediatrician's advice in matters and methods of feeding is always a risk.

Mothers of only children probably create more feeding problems by being overanxious and overinsistent than by being overindulgent. We have watched more than one mother of an Only sitting in front of him and coaxing and coaxing him to eat his puréed vegetables while he turned his head away, pushed the spoon back, and shoved the plate off onto the floor. We've seen a mother insist that an Only drink his milk and, when he stubbornly refused, punish him severely. He still won't drink milk.

Dr. Paul Williamson, of the American Academy of General Practice, says mothers should remember that children eat less per pound as they grow older, that they are sometimes not hungry, and that when they are badgered about eating they rebel and won't eat at all. The last observation lends point to the advice which many pediatricians give. Set an attractive course before the child and leave him. Don't insist that he eat if he doesn't want to, but don't give him dessert until he has finished the earlier course. Don't feed him between meals. He will eat when he is hungry.

The modern pediatrician is an expert not only in diet but in behavior. Mothers need the expert's advice and should follow it. But they can prevent any good result if they hang anxiously over their child. A pertinent study shows that, when mothers work, their children rarely present feeding problems.

Negativism

Most children go through periods of saying "NO!" especially when they are going on 3. An older child who says "No" occasionally is like the child who sometimes refuses to eat: he may have a good reason and his refusal should be honored. But if he says "NO!" to everything, the cause may well be too strict control.

The child who is subjected to what a famous psychiatrist, the late J. S. Plant, described as a "torrent of parental questions and directions" has to develop a negative reaction to save himself. "NO!" is his best life preserver.

Only children are certainly exposed to the full force of the parental torrent if it is flowing, and often to a spate of commands from grandparents, uncles, and aunts as well. Anne Ward ("The Only Child," *Smith College Studies in Social Work,* Vol. I, 1930-31) found that negativism was most frequent in those Onlies who lived with several grown-ups. Certainly the habit of saying "NO!" disappears, as Plant observed, when it is possible "to still the torrent."

At the risk of provoking a negative reaction in the reader, we offer several directions for mitigating negativism. First, be sure that you are not controlling the child's every move with questions and directions. If you are sure you are not, you can do one of two things. You can accept the child's refusal in such a way that he suffers the natural consequences of it; if he refuses to put away his toys and come to supper, you can go ahead with supper and let him go without or be content with plain bread and milk. Or you can drop everything you are doing and see your order obeyed. You certainly should not go on repeating an order in a nagging fashion. Negativism can be cured, as it can be prevented, by parental firmness and consistency.

Temper Tantrums

Temper tantrums are said to be characteristic of only children. They are certainly characteristic of spoiled and indulged children. But the seriousness of tantrums depends on the age of the child. All young children have them. Like other forms of behavior, tantrums rise and fall in frequency at different ages. There seem to be peaks at about the age of 2 and at about 4. After 4, tantrums should begin to be less frequent, and they should practically disappear by the age of 10.

Tantrums usually start when a child is denied some wish. The child's inborn aggressiveness makes him try to get his own way even in the face of parental disapproval. He works up a lot of energy to accomplish his purpose. When he is thwarted so he cannot apply this energy directly, he releases it in a blind rage. There is some method in his madness. Many a poor boxer, frustrated by the skill of his opponent, has hit out in wrath and scored a victory with a lucky blow. Many a child has obtained his goal by throwing a tantrum, when calmer methods would have gained him nothing.

No child of any age should be allowed to gain his end by means of a tantrum. If he does, he'll soon explode like an atom bomb whenever he can't have what he wants. When he has a tantrum, he should be helped to recover himself as quickly as possible. The best method is to redirect his energy by giving him some legitimate way to expend it. A young child can be picked up and joked with. A good laugh is always an excellent way to ease tension. When a child seems involved in a chain reaction that he cannot stop, it may be necessary to shock him back to his senses by dashing cold water in his face or giving him a sharp slap on the buttocks. The purpose is not to punish him but to help him refocus. Punishment is worse than useless, because attack causes counterattack and anger rouses anger. Sometimes, when you know what is troubling a child, you can help him ease the tension by putting his feelings into words for him: "I know. You're mad at me because I won't let you have a cooky." Sometimes isolation is the best solution. It lets the child exhaust his rage in private and is perhaps the easiest procedure for the child and everyone else.

Parents who are firm and consistent about not giving in to a tantrum are doing what is best for the child. They are helping him learn to control his temper and to use his energy constructively. Parents who try to win peace by giving in are doomed to failure. They can never give the spoiled child enough, for the more they give, the more the child will want. The moon will still be in the sky.

Attention-Seeking

A teen-age Only volunteered the statement: "Only children are so used to attention that if they can't get it one way they will in another." Her mother chipped in, quite rightly, that this is no longer true of this particular girl. But it is true of some Onlies—and not all of them children.

It is a common fate of an only child to be with his mother when callers come and to be taken calling. The results can be embarrassing for the mother and bad for the child. The adults may form an admiring circle and vie with each other for the favor of a smile or word or hug from the child. Or they may try to talk to each other while the child squirms, pouts, and interrupts.

One mother, taking her Only with her on a call, thought she would solve the problem by providing pad and pencil. The child sat perhaps a minute gravely watching the group of four adults. Then he dropped pad and pencil, went over to his mother, and began tugging at her sleeve. She sent him back to his chair. In thirty seconds he was at her side again. The shuttling continued, faster and faster. The mother grew crosser and crosser, and her voice sharper and sharper. The child began to whine about going home. Finally the hostess picked up the pad, took the child to one side, and began to draw pictures for him. Sweet silence fell on the room.

Of course, children do deserve attention. The need for recognition is one of the main emotional needs. It must be satisfied in a healthy way if a child is to develop a healthy personality. But attention forced for attention's sake is not healthy. A child who draws a good picture thrives on praise. A child who bullies an adult into drawing a picture for him may not be hurt—we've been known to purchase peace this way ourselves—but again he may be. He may be learning to force recognition by being unpleasant.

A mother alone with a child can ignore nuisance-making bids for attention and give due recognition for behavior she really likes. If she uses this combination the nuisance soon abates and the child learns how to conduct himself when he's with adults, as he must often be. But when a child hasn't learned and continues to demand attention, he's pretty sure to have his way. The solution at home is to have safe places for the child to play indoors and out and have him play there when adults come to call. As for taking the child calling on other people: don't, unless you know there will be children or a dog for him to play with or unless you are very sure he can and will amuse himself with a book or paper and pencil or a toy. Even then the risk that your friends will gush should give you pause.

The Submissive Child

When a child is quiet and submissive to directions, parents and the parents' friends say, "What a good child he is." The psychologist, however, regards extreme submissiveness as a danger sign; he would rather see a child sometimes inconvenience others by trying to get his own way than to see him always do what he is told.

One Only, a girl aged 7, seemed to her teacher to be dangerously quiet and withdrawing. The teacher consulted a friend of the girl's family. "Why," said the friend, "she's the sweetest, best-behaved little girl I ever knew. I took a week-end tour with her mother, her aunt, and her. I was afraid one child with so many grownups would be a pest. Do you know she never got in the way at all—never wandered off, never asked any of us to let her have or do anything special. She always did just what she was told. She was plain sweet and smiling for three whole days."

The child who always does what he is told, especially if he is always told what to do, is not learning to meet and overcome obstacles. As long as there is an experienced adult at hand on whom he can depend for directions, he does not suffer. But life is full of many obstacles against which the individual must struggle by himself. He must learn to make plans and decisions for himself. If he is deficient in aggressiveness, if he cannot care for himself, he may be trampled to death in the rush of life.

When the submissive child meets competition from other children and when he finds himself faced with an unusually difficult assignment in school, he gives up very easily. He may take refuge in daydreaming. In his dreams the rewards and pleasures of life are heaped on him. There is no need to make choices. He runs no risk. He has no fear of failure. In extreme cases the dream is so much more attractive than the world that the child begins to live in the dream and refuses to return to meet the painful demands of everyday life.

Submissiveness is quite likely to result when a child is severely dominated. If his parents (or either parent) subject him to overstrict control he gets the habit of submitting. The only child is particularly liable to domination. There is no other child to distract the parents' attention or to take their time, so they are free to supervise him every minute. If the dominating behavior is due to some past experience, if a parent is venting long-suppressed emotions, the Only bears the brunt and continues to bear it. Moreover, the Only is so much with adults in situations where he lacks the knowledge and experience to make any decisions for himself that he becomes accustomed to leaving all positive action to others.

Luckily most children, including the vast majority of Onlies, are neither overindulged nor dominated, neither spoiled nor submissive. Their parents have managed to maintain a good balance and have not been either too permissive or too strict. The children have learned to be aggressive when aggression is called for and conforming when circumstances demand. The child who remains timid and withdrawing, especially if he spends hours in daydreaming, needs expert help.

Masturbation

The mother of an only child is with him so much that she is likely to be aware of how much he handles his genitals.

Very young children, both boys and girls, handle their genitals just as naturally as they do their toes. They find the sensation pleasant, and normally continue to touch or rub themselves occasionally. Practically all boys and the majority of girls sooner or later masturbate to the point of orgasm. Physiologists, psychologists, and psychiatrists are certain that masturbation in itself does no harm, physical, mental, or emotional.

Parents may be so upset by seeing a child masturbate ("I caught him at it") that they may punish the child severely. They may threaten to cut off a boy's penis, or to burn a girl's finger. They may tell the child that if masturbation continues there will be all kinds of evil results, including insanity and impotence. The child usually continues to masturbate, but he is so worried by what he is doing that he may make himself emotionally sick.

Children may turn to masturbation, as they do to thumb-sucking, as a means of solace when they are upset by difficult situations. The masturbation may become the child's only pleasure and be indulged in so constantly as to exclude other activities. Van Krevelen thinks excessive masturbation especially likely to occur among only girls because they face a special difficulty in resolving the Oedipus complex. In any case, excessive masturbation should be recognized as a symptom, and an attempt made to discover and remove the cause.

One Only, whose parents were getting a divorce, went to visit his grandparents. His grandmother reports that when he first arrived "he handled himself all day long," but, as he learned he was loved and safe, he masturbated less and less until he practically stopped.

Parents should be careful not to scold, threaten, or punish a child for handling genitals or masturbating. They should be sure that the child has plenty of interesting things to do and, as he grows older, that he has plenty of friends of both sexes. They should try to be sure that he is not badly worried or emotionally upset, and especially sure that he does not feel unloved and unwanted. When a child who is masturbating to excess or in public does not respond to these measures, he should be taken to a child-guidance clinic.

A psychologist on the staff of a clinic reports: "I was asked to test Gerry because he would never finish his work, worked carelessly, didn't get along with other children, and frequently masturbated in class. He's a nice-looking boy of 9 in Grade III. Tests showed that his intelligence was normal and more than adequate for the work of his grade. During the test I noticed that he bit his nails constantly; they were already chewed to the quick. He was cocky in a way that made me sure he was on the defensive. Investigation in the home showed that he is an only child. His father died soon after he was born. His mother went to work to support the family. Gerry's grandmother and aunt live in the house. Gerry's mother is inclined to belittle him. Asked about his health, she said, 'He's allergic.' 'To what?' 'Work.' " Gerry was helped by a summer camp and by the school social worker's showing his mother that Gerry would behave better if he were praised for what he did well instead of scolded for what he did badly.

"Real Trouble in Our House"

One tense, worried, overactive, unpredictable Only, aged 6, began a conversation with the remark, "You know, we've got real trouble in our house. My father is a very sick man."

The close association of an only child with his parents inevitably gives him a rather full knowledge of the family problems. Sick mothers or fathers, fathers who are actually unemployed or in danger of losing their jobs, heavy family debts, and harsh newspaper criticism of a father who is a public official are some of the burdens about which we have found young only children worrying. To be sure, non-Onlies are subject to similar misfortunes and suffer grievously in the circumstances. But the Only has no one his own age to share his troubles or to distract him, perhaps even to keep him so busy that he doesn't sense his parents' anxiety.

Troubles cannot be kept hidden from the only child, perhaps not from any child. Preventing the child from overhearing conversations might be possible, but a wife whose husband is a very sick man can hardly hide her worry. The child senses this and begins to worry too. Often the child's worry is not about the possible death of the parent, but about what will become of the child if the worst happens. Several of our adult Onlies say that as children they were filled with fear of what would happen if both father and mother died and they were left all alone. The only child in this instance certainly misses the security, the feeling of belonging, and the conviction of support which siblings give each other.

Death or divorce, actual or feared, are unfortunate circumstances in the lives of many only children (see Chapter XIII). The strain on the child is extreme, but it does not necessarily break him. If a parent, in the face of all his own grief and disturbance, can take time to make clear to the child that the child will not be abandoned, all may be well. The more concrete the plans for the child's future and the more chance he has to grow familiar with them, the better.

VII.

Adjustment in the Early Years of School

ONE September, a *New Yorker* cover showed a little girl sallying forth to school. Her mother stands on the porch watching her. The girl, wearing a bright red coat, radiates cheerful excitement. She's off on her own without a backward glance. But the mother is the expression of woe. She is dressed in solid black. A ragged doll droops from her hand. She waves a hand forlornly; the child looks ahead to the school, waves gaily but doesn't look back.

Starting school carries, for an American child, the portents of a primitive tribe's rites of initiation. It marks the transition from infancy to childhood. It signalizes the first break with the family. From now on the child is a part of the tribe. No wonder the event looms large in prospect, in passing, and in retrospect.

Much depends on whether a child starts school as a first-grader, aged about 6, a kindergartner, aged about 5, or in nursery school, aged 4 or under. Both theory and practical experience indicate that the gradual initiation into school life which a good nursery school provides is somewhat better for all children and much better for only children than the sharp break which occurs when the child goes directly into first grade. Starting in kindergarten is better than starting in first grade, but not as good as starting in nursery school.

Nursery School and Kindergarten

The decision as to when a child should go to nursery school hinges largely on what school is available. The good school will not accept a child who is too immature to profit from its program. Unfortunately there are not good nursery schools (or even kindergartens) in all communities.

The essentials of a good nursery school are: (1) Professionally trained teachers who are emotionally mature, wholesome people. The head teacher should have had several years of experience. (2) An adequate staff. The maximum number of children a teacher handles at one time should be limited to six 2-year-olds, eight 3-year-olds, or ten 4-year-olds. (3) A fire-safe building and ample safe outdoor play space. (4) A high standard of cleanliness for floors, toilets, and kitchen. (5) Provision for frequent consultation with parents, both as individuals and in groups.

All of these requirements cost money. Tuition in the good private school runs to $500 or more a year. Few families feel they can afford this. The result is a rapid growth of cooperative nursery schools. A cooperative school is a big advantage to the parents of an only child because it brings them into contact with other parents of growing children and gives them an opportunity to exchange experiences and information. But a cooperative needs more than the good intentions of a small group of inexperienced mothers. There is still need for a professionally trained teacher, and this teacher should have had experience in a cooperative.

Granted a good school that will accept a particular 2-year-old, parents who know that their child is going to be an Only should consider starting him even at this early age. There is some professional doubt whether most 2-year-olds are ready even for the attenuated program—an hour or two a week—which is customary for this age. But the early start sets a healthy precedent of separation, however brief, of parent and child and so paves the way for the longer and longer periods which will occur in the years to come. Nursery school gives a 2-year-old experience in being with other children at a time when playmates may be hard to find and play is hard to supervise. The good teacher knows, as most young parents cannot, what to expect of a group of 2-year-olds. She knows how to encourage both self-reliance and cooperation and to redirect behavior that might otherwise develop into misbehavior.

Parents of an only child who is 3 or 4 certainly do better to send him to a good nursery school than to wait to start him off in kindergarten or first grade. Separation, even for a few hours each day, safeguards him against overprotection. Since he lacks a younger sibling to push him—or an older sib to pull him—into independence, he may develop a habit of looking to his mother for help in many things which he should be doing for himself. The longer he remains dependent the more chance there is that he will dislike doing things for himself when he finally does start school. He may then recoil, run back to his mother, and grow up a "mamma's boy." The child who goes to nursery school learns to do for himself. He learns to like other children and may "love" his teacher.

Another advantage in nursery school for the only child is that there will probably be a good many other Onlies in the group. He is not thought of as in any way different from the other children either by them or by the teacher. If Onliness is due to divorce or to death, the other children are not likely to make unthinking and cruel remarks, and by the time they might, the Only is already an accepted member of the group. But a first-grader may be put in the position of the boy who came home and told his divorced mother, "They said my father ran away from you and me. I told them he took a taxi."

The only child, lacking experience in compulsory companionship, often has a rough time if he starts school with first grade, because the group is large and the hours long and because the curriculum, especially reading, may place a strain on him. If most of the other pupils in the class went to kindergarten together he is at a further disadvantage, because they already know each other and he feels excluded from the group. The child who has been to nursery school or kindergarten, like the one brought up in a large family, already knows how to stand up for himself boldly in case of need and how to yield when he must. He knows how to get along with other children, even the ones he may not like very well. In brief, he's already somewhat wise in the ways of the world.

Detailed research into the benefits which Onlies receive from nursery school has been made by van Krevelen. He studied 187 only children in Rotterdam elementary schools. Half of these had been to nursery school and half had not. The nursery-school graduates made notably better adjustments in their schoolwork and in their relations with other children than did those who entered elementary school direct.

Our case histories show that the school is often the agency of reform. A child who has been babied at home by overprotective parents adjusts with difficulty to a situation where he is not the center of attention and cannot have his every wish fulfilled. But, like all human beings, the only child has a desire to conform. This makes him try to be a regular fellow, to take his turn, to put up with pain and disappointment like a good sport. When he fails, the other pupils are not slow to let him know about it.

Off to a Good Start

There are many things which the parents, and particularly the mother, of an only child can do to help him off to a good start in school, whether it's nursery school or later.

Visit the school some months before the child is going to enter. Talk with the principal to be sure you understand all the regulations about age of entrance, district lines, health certificates, and vaccination certificates. Find out if there is a PTA and, if there is, join it. Many school systems have what they call a "round-up" in June for all children scheduled to start school in September. This usually includes a physical examination. Volunteer your services in connection with the round-up. Take your child to the round-up even if he's had a recent examination by his own doctor. Seeing the other children who are going to start school with him will help set his mind for it.

Your child's attitude toward starting school will depend somewhat on whether he has friends and neighbors a little older who are already attending. If he has, or if his friends have older siblings in school, he will look forward to the time when he can go. But, lacking this vicarious experience, he may be quite apprehensive. Explain school to the child simply. Talk to him occasionally about his going, being sure to speak of it as something he will like. Don't give him the idea that you are pushing him out to have more time for yourself. It's a good idea to mention some things you will enjoy doing together in the afternoon after school.

Take the child to visit the school and let him see what it's like. Have him meet his teacher. If he has friends who are going to be in the same class, you might arrange to take him to visit the school when one of them will be visiting with his mother. Study the clothing which the other children wear. An only child is likely to have much better clothing than other children because his parents can afford it and because there are no hand-me-downs. He is also likely to be more careful of good clothes than other children because he has been more exposed to adult attitudes. But clothes-consciousness may keep an Only from sharing rough-

and-tumble play with his contemporaries. He may be unwilling to play in the dirt or even with finger paints in
school. Experiences in rough play and with dirt are good
antidotes to the apartness, the lonely sense of being different, from which some Onlies suffer. So dress him in faded
jeans and a sweat shirt if that is what other children are
wearing.

All of these activities will help you set your own mind for
the break. If you are grieving over the change, or if you are
tense and worried, the child will begin to worry too. Remembering your own school days and watching the work
of the teacher who will have your child are good means of
reassuring yourself.

When registering your child, give the principal and
teacher all the information which they request. For example, if a kindergarten child can't button himself up after
going to the toilet, the teacher should know it. Don't let a
false pride lead you to make claims for the child that he
cannot make good.

Nursery schools expect the mother to accompany the
child to school for the first several days and to stay until
the child is used to his new situation. In some cases, kindergarten teachers will suggest that a mother stay with the
child for a few sessions. Be guided by the teacher's advice
as to when to let the child go to school without you. *Do not
stay at the school if the teacher advises against it.*

Whether you accompany a first-grader to school or not
depends largely on the conditions along the route he must
take. Generally you will go with him the first day. If traffic
conditions are bad, take care to work out with him the best
route and to teach him exactly where he is to cross streets
and how. Do not continue to accompany a child to and
from school when the other children of his age in your
neighborhood are going alone. Your going with him when

the others are on their own exposes him to harsh teasing, and the older he is the more he will suffer. Unwillingness to let a child walk alone to and from school over a route which other parents think safe is one of the indications of overprotection. Moreover, it keeps the child from developing responsibility for himself and may actually increase the danger that he will later be run over. That young children do manage to go to and from school alone is evident. In one suburban school which we checked there are 73 children in the kindergarten, including 10 Onlies; just 6 of the 73 are regularly brought to school by an adult, and none of these is an Only. Checks on city schools show smaller percentages of children who are brought to school, presumably because distances are shorter and crossings are protected, though traffic is heavier. We know one 5-year-old who proudly takes a regular bus home each day. He hasn't lost his fare yet. On the day when he spent it for candy, he trudged the three quarters of a mile from school to house without ill effects.

Grade I

Only children, because of their close association with adults, are frequently ahead of their age mates in the number of words which they know and can use, and in reading ability. There is, therefore, a temptation to enter an only child in Grade I when he is still very young, or even to ask to have him skip Grade I. Both steps are dangerous. If the Only's superiority is due more to association with adults than to native intelligence, he will find before long that he can't keep up. Even if he has superior intelligence, he may be too immature physically and socially to mix well with other children. Then he may seek recognition by devoting himself to his studies. He may become an intellectual snob, and that is not a happy fate. We are not against a bright student's skipping, but we think he should wait until he has proved his ability to get along with other children. The following case is pertinent:

One of our Onlies, a very bright boy aged 6 years, was already reading well. His mother thought of Grade I as being mainly concerned with reading and thought her son could skip it. The school supervisor strongly recommended that he shouldn't, and the mother agreed. The first-grade teacher reported at the end of the first week, "He walks around among the other children like the absent-minded professor." He much preferred talking with the teacher to working and playing with the children. But during the year he learned that there were things other children could do better than he. He developed well physically and his co-ordination improved. He was a bookish child from a bookish family, but the curriculum's emphasis on the local community and the teacher's emphasis on group work combined to put him in closer touch with reality. His mother remarked, "I had no idea there were so many things to learn in first grade." At the end of the year he was promoted to Grade III, and made a good adjustment there.

The Precocious Child

There is undoubtedly a danger that the precocious child will be unpopular with his contemporaries, but many of our case histories of Onlies which describe the children as "very mature" or "quite grown-up" state that these children are well-liked by their playmates. For example, a bright 6-year-old in Grade I is described by her teacher as "a very stable, sensible, mature child who assumes independent responsibility well. She is extremely capable—a leader. Further she is very popular with other children, being outgoing and friendly." An 11-year-old boy in Grade V, who spends over-much time with adults and reflects this in both manner and speech, nonetheless "gets along well with other children.

Though shy, he makes friends quickly. He is far more popular than he realizes. He is, however, inclined to withdraw and daydreams much of the time."

Luckily the very bright child can apply his superior intelligence to problems in human relations as well as to those of arithmetic. A teacher tells of an 8-year-old boy in Grade III who has a mental age of 15 and an IQ of 153. He had been very slow to make any friends. On the school playground he was always trying to talk with the teacher rather than play games with the other children. To a child of his intelligence a teacher is more interesting than children. The teacher had to work hard to teach him to play with his peers. How well she succeeded is shown by the conclusion of her report: "He has fallen in love with a bright girl in the class. They plan to be married when they grow up. They are going to have seven children and live on a farm."

The Misfits

The adjustment of only children to school has been the subject of many studies. Parents can take comfort in the fact that several of these studies show that only children as a group do well in school. R. B. Guilford and D. A. Worcester (*Pedagogical Seminary*, 1930, Vol. 38, pp. 411-426) compared 21 only children aged 11-15 with 141 children of the same age who had siblings. They found the Onlies superior in 13 of 14 measures, namely, IQ, marks, courtesy, truth, industry, initiative, self-control, cooperation, dependability, health, personal order and cleanliness, law and order, and fairness, but very slightly inferior in "voluntary participation in extracurricular activities." Other recent studies have reached the conclusion that "only children probably differ little or at all from those with siblings."

. But the wise parent does not take any child's school adjustment for granted. He wants to know as soon as possible if anything is going wrong. He wants to be aware of causes of difficulties and to know what remedies to apply.

Van Krevelen found that when Onlies first start school they suffer from inexperience in rough-and-tumble play and in group contacts. He says they are timid and polite and well-liked by the teacher for these qualities, which, however, make them less-desired comrades for other children. They do not take teasing well and therefore are subject to a great deal of it. But as they progress through school, Onlies show an "increasing betterment in accommodation." They take teasing better, don't want their own way so much, and learn to get along well with others. Van Krevelen thinks that when an Only has had to fight himself to overcome his difficulties in the early grades, he later has an advantage over non-Onlies who are still trying to find themselves.

Girls adjust to school quicker than boys, and girl Onlies quicker than boy Onlies. In one of our sets of school histories, half of the boy Onlies are characterized by their teachers as immature, but merely one-sixth of the girl Onlies are so described. Dr. Edith Davis has found that teachers frequently call boy Onlies spoiled, queer, and nervous, but very generally speak of girl Onlies as well-adjusted and normal.

Ward, in her study of the behavior problems of 100 only children (73 boys, 27 girls) who had been referred to child-guidance clinics, tried to discover what the causes of their difficulties were. She found that these clinic Onlies had much the same problems as other clinic children except that they had more difficulties with schoolwork. These school troubles, she says, cannot be accounted for by intelligence, age, or grade placement because there is nothing unusual about the children in these respects. She concludes that her clinic Onlies were unaccustomed to being with a group, were used to getting help when faced with hard tasks, and were used to being the center of attention and therefore resorted to attention-getting behavior or to daydreaming. She finds that their home backgrounds are marked by overprotection and by overambitious parents. The children whose school behavior was bad were likely to be children of parents who had little outside social life or to come from homes in which several adults lived. Children who were unpopular were likely to come from homes where there were few outside contacts and where they were overprotected.

Our case histories of Onlies show that school difficulties, particularly those due to immaturity, are likely to occur when the child is overprotected. We also find several cases in which the trouble can be traced to indirect factors connected with Onliness, especially to homes broken by death or divorce or to the poor health of one of the parents.

When home conditions are responsible for a child's difficulties in school, the parents themselves may be the last to recognize the fact. They may blame the school, particularly if they are inclined to overprotect the child. They may blame other children who, they say, are leading their child into trouble. They may even blame the child himself. Sometimes one parent may see that the other is being something less than wise. In such a case, the parent who sees that all is not going well with the child has an obligation to all concerned. He cannot trust to the child's outgrowing his difficulties, but must take the initiative in seeking help and continue to work at the problem until it is solved.

Parents who are alert for signs that a child is not adjusting well in his first months at school can do much to keep his problem from developing serious proportions.

Signs of Trouble

A good, well-trained, experienced teacher quickly spots the children in her room who are not adjusting well. Here is a classification of the indications of poor adjustment which teachers mention in our school histories of only children.

Too aggressive. Bossy, fights, hits others, causes trouble on the bus, seeks attention, too talkative.

Withdrawing. Daydreams, never joins the group, doesn't join in games and sports, never volunteers in class, doesn't talk much with other children, timid, fearful, shy.

Immature. Talks baby talk, sucks thumb, can't button buttons, cries easily, easily upset.

Poor in schoolwork. Distractible, doesn't follow directions, gives up easily, won't try hard tasks, below academic standard of his intelligence, especially in reading or arithmetic.

Socially unadjusted. Rejected by the group, teased a lot and can't take it, silly, poor in games, conceited, ignores others' rights, doesn't share.

(We hasten to add that our reports from schools also speak well of many Onlies. Some of the terms used are: leader, friendly, cooperative, self-reliant, well-liked, courteous, intellectually curious, excellent student.)

A teacher may or may not give a child's parents early notice that all is not going perfectly. Too many teachers have to handle excessively large classes and feel they have not the time and strength to write notes or make calls. Being human, teachers are inclined to postpone taking action to meet a problem that may solve itself—as the school problems of Onlies frequently do. And some teachers dread the reaction of parents to anything that might be taken as a criticism of a child. In view of these circumstances, a parent ought to visit the school a month or six weeks after school starts each year and get a first-hand report from the child's teacher. The parent who visits school runs the risk of being thought fussy and overprotective, but this is quickly nullified by willingness to listen to the teacher and to accept her recommendations.

The way a child talks to his parents about school gives some indication of how well he is doing. School is an exciting adventure and pretty much the center of the child's life. Failure to answer such questions as, "What did you do in school today?" especially when the silence is accompanied by a marked increase in demand for love, is a bad sign. So also is excessive boasting. A child can be forgiven a considerable degree of exaggeration, but lies about his own prowess and tattling of other children's misdeeds are both signs of insecurity. The child is trying to bolster the parents' estimation of him. The best treatment is to ignore the boasts or tales, direct the conversation along another line, and try to make the child feel more secure. You can, for example, praise him for something you sincerely like that he has done really well, particularly any incident of good sportsmanship that you have witnessed.

Psychosomatic headaches, vomiting, and other ailments that afford an excuse for not going to school on Monday morning or any other day, or for getting sent home from school, require attention. Try to start the child talking about his troubles and let him talk them out. Visit the school and see what suggestions the teacher can make. But don't let such illnesses continue to serve as an excuse. If you do, they may become chronic. One mother reports that she didn't dare send her son back to school with a temperature, even though she suspected it was emotional. So she let him stay home that afternoon, and next morning went into his room early, waked him up, and took his temperature before he could start thinking. It was, as she had hoped, normal, and she packed him off promptly.

Sometimes a child will beg or steal candy, or money to

buy candy, to take to school and give to other children. This is not pure generosity, but an attempt to buy popularity, and so a sign that the child is not being welcomed for his own sake. He needs to be built up in other ways and particularly to be encouraged to take an interest in games.

Most children, at least by the time they are 7, will want to bring their new friends home to play with them. If an only child does not, his parents should suggest it. They probably have more play space available than families with more children. If the child takes the initiative, by all means encourage him. When a child's classmates are out-of-school friends, his troubles are not likely to be serious in school or out.

Overambitious Parents

Overambitious parents drive many an Only to desperation. The child is the parents' one connection with the future. They say that they want him to have everything that they did not have. Maybe they have refrained from having more children so they can give the Only every advantage. They hope to see the Only fulfill all their unfulfilled ambitions. They look forward to basking in the glow of his fame. Any failure in school, especially any shortcoming in academic achievement, seems to them a betrayal. They impress the child with the idea that if he is not first in his class he is letting them down. The child may react by rebelling, especially if he is actually not above average in intelligence. Or, if he has some ability and is the type which cannot brook competition, he may accept his parents' point of view and sacrifice everything to make the honor roll.

One of our adult Onlies remembers how this kind of pressure affected her. She says, "I always had to be at the top. I couldn't stand anyone else near me. If I thought a teacher didn't like me best I'd pout and not speak to her for days. In my small rural elementary school I was always at the top, but when I went to college the competition was too stiff. I drove myself into a nervous breakdown."

The first balance to parental overambition is a realistic appraisal of the child's abilities. The surest way to secure this is to have the child given an individual test by a qualified psychologist. But a parent who is willing to admit that a child's progress may be in line with his intelligence and that slow progress is not just a matter of lack of work can make a pretty shrewd guess by watching how his child does in school and by talking with his teacher. We have discussed the subject at length in our book *Bright Children*.

Parents who feel that a child is not doing all he should in school are quite likely to try to help him at home. This is fine if it is done with the teacher's approval and by methods which fit in with the methods of the school. Otherwise there is danger of confusing the child. And sometimes overambitious or overprotective parents fall into the habit of doing all a child's homework for him or even getting copies of his schoolbooks and tutoring him in advance. They defeat their own purpose because they are teaching him to depend on them rather than on himself. He may parrot their answers but lack understanding because he has not worked through the subject matter for himself.

Of course a child who is not learning as well as a child of his ability should, needs help. The parents, cooperating with the teacher, should try to find out where the trouble lies. Sometimes the difficulty is hard to locate but easy to correct. One very bright only child had been to both nursery school and kindergarten, liked her classmates and teachers, and had done well. She went into Grade I and failed entirely to learn to read. A psychologist was consulted. He talked with the child awhile and said, "She doesn't realize that first grade is something different. Explain to her *why* she should learn to read and that play comes second, and watch what happens." Now, at 9, reading is one of the child's favorite recreations.

Physical Handicaps

On analyzing our materials we are struck by the fact that, as in the cases of so many children who do badly in school, a number of our Onlies whose academic progress has not been satisfactory are actually in poor health and that parents and teachers have not handled all of them wisely. The case of Mason shows how poor health can be both a handicap in itself and a means of aggravating other adverse factors.

Mason was born after a prolonged labor. He had a head injury and the doctors doubted if he would live. He was very slow in learning to walk, and when he started kindergarten at the age of 5 he still had very poor muscular control and coordination. But he had learned to talk quite young and spoke well. His kindergarten teacher reported that he was immature and small for his age and tended to watch others instead of carrying on any activity of his own. The school physical examination showed he had defective vision. His family took him to an oculist, who prescribed glasses. The visual defect is still serious, and Mason has to wear his glasses all of the time. In Grade I he was said to be dependent on others and inattentive, but he learned to read quickly, and at the end of the year a standard test showed him reading two years ahead of his age and grade level. From Grade II on, Mason's academic achievement went slowly downhill. His mother visited school occasionally and was said to be understanding and cooperative. His father was reported as "indulgent but he often censures the boy for lack of progress. Mason then gets upset nervously and can do no work."

According to his eighth-grade teacher, Mason's physical

handicaps led to his being indulged and protected at home and at school. "His teachers are sorry for him and give him every consideration." The report for the ninth grade reads, "He demands a maximum of attention to complete a minimum of work . . . if corrected, he trembles and may cry." A high-school teacher reported, "He has an abnormal desire to please and becomes exceedingly disturbed at even a minor correction."

Mason's family, particularly his father, had expected him to go to college and had saved enough money to pay for his college tuition. But his low grades ruled him out of the college-preparatory course. He took a general course. Now, at the age of 20, he holds a minor job in an office.

There can be no doubt about Mason's physical handicaps, but one wonders if his parents and teachers did all they could to help him overcome them. His school career and the tests he took showed that it was not lack of intelligence nor yet poor vision that kept him from doing well, but rather a tendency to depend on others. There is more than a chance that if Mason's parents had handled him with loving matter-of-factness instead of indulgence he would have learned to take correction. (Spock, in *The Pocket Book of Baby and Child Care,* gives excellent advice about how to handle invalid and handicapped children.) Mason's father, instead of censuring failure, could have consistently tried to build him up by helping him to do better what he could do well. The teachers, instead of being sorry for him, might tactfully have directed him into group activities where he could hold his own. No one can say whether care of this type would have made either Mason or his parents happier. We can say that a great many individuals, including many Onlies, have succeeded despite much worse handicaps than Mason had.

VIII.

Playmates and Friends

ONE of our best-adjusted Onlies says, "I grew up with eight cousins, including one who was also an Only and my best friend." The mother of a thriving 17-year-old Only says, "From the very beginning we've made strenuous efforts to provide playmates. I remember how much my sister meant to me."

No matter how hard the parents of an Only strive to provide him with playmates and friends and to play with him themselves to make up for the lack of brothers and sisters, he is bound to be more alone than the child in a larger family. For example, an only child who comes in from play at dark, or at any time when his friends are called to their homes, may find his mother hurrying to get supper and his father not yet home from work. He is thrown on his own resources. Often the only child comes home to an empty house, particularly if both his parents work.

Moreover the only child can be lonely, can feel apart, even when his parents are present and trying their best to be good companions. A mother of an Only says: "Children live in a world of their own. Parents cannot share their feelings, their joys and sorrows, in the same way that brothers and sisters do. I can think back to my own childhood and remember the wild and shrieking excitement of running in to see our Christmas tree and Christmas stockings with my brothers." An adult, who was herself an only child, remembers going to a friend's house for Christmas

Eve dinner and her envy of the fun the large family had. She adds, "They all had gifts for me and were as nice as they could be and I never felt so lonely in my life."

The joy of the adult, on festive occasions, is in the child's pleasure. The adult is not shrieking with excitement. He does not share the child's point of view. The child is alone in his feelings.

The only child is even more alone in his feelings of sorrow than of joy, especially when his sorrow is over being blamed for something. Misery loves company and he has no company. He must accept the parents' point of view. If he is in disgrace, he is all alone in his disgrace.

Even when he is at school or playing with friends, the Only is likely to feel lonely because he lacks the support of brothers or sisters. A boy or girl with older siblings who have been to the same school, especially if they still share the same playground, has a sense of security. An older brother may tease and even beat up his younger brother without mercy but be quick to come to his defense against an outsider. An Only who sees this happen (particularly if he is the outsider) may very well think he has been cheated. He doesn't know or doesn't stop to think about all the times the brothers fight each other or how difficult it may be to live up to—or live down—an older brother's reputation.

Imaginary Playmates

One of the earliest articles on only children implied that loneliness made them invent imaginary playmates, and this assertion has since been repeated without challenge in article after article. But as far as we can discover, only children are no more likely to have imaginary playmates than are other children. The most thorough investigation of imaginary playmates which we know is that by E. B. Hurlock and M. Burstein. They questioned 701 high-school and college students and discovered that 31 per cent of the women and 23 per cent of the men remembered having invented a playmate. The number of other children in the family made no difference in the case of either the women or the men. The child with brothers and sisters was just as likely to invent a companion as was the only child. Few of these students could explain how they had come to think up their friend. Usually the imaginary child just suddenly appeared. Sometimes the imaginary child could be traced to a story or picture. About one fifth of those with imaginary playmates thought loneliness was a contributing cause in the situation.

In any event, parents whose child has an imaginary playmate need not worry. The phenomenon is very common and does no harm.

Only children do often learn to tell themselves stories and, in general, to depend on their own imagination for amusement and comfort. This can be an advantage. Van Krevelen points out that many of the great imaginative writers were only children.

Playmates Are Important

Free and independent play with other children is certainly the best means of providing any child with the experiences which teach him to get along with people. Such play should be in addition to play with parents, supervised play with other children, and play alone. All of these are good for a child in themselves and as a step to self-confidence in personal relationships, but in time children must be left to themselves to manage themselves.

If a child is to fulfill his emotional need for group membership, he must have the satisfaction of knowing that he is accepted for himself and as himself by his peers. He must weather the storms that rise during free play among children: the persistent teasing, the brutal criticism, the fights, and the temporary exclusions. He must learn to compete for his due share of privileges and of honors. He must learn fortitude in the face of pain and disappointment, and endurance in the face of difficulties. He has to find out the values that children, like their elders, attach to courage, initiative, and generosity. He has to learn to tolerate the idiosyncrasies of others. He has to be a good sport, eager to win but able to lose gracefully. He must learn "to feel right about other people," a feeling which the National Association for Mental Health says is characteristic of the mentally healthy individual.

It's Harder for an Only

The only child is likely to be lacking in experience with other children, partly because he has no forced association with brothers and sisters, and partly because his parents get in his way. A few parents do this deliberately because they are afraid to let a child play with other children. Many keep a child to themselves without thinking that they are robbing him of companionship with his age mates. Whatever the cause, the number of Onlies who have trouble learning to associate with other children when they first go to school shows that an Only may be under an initial handicap in making friends.

Stages in Social Development

A knowledge of what to expect in a child's social development aids parents in helping a child make friends and benefit from friendships. Parents of first and only children are prone to expect too much too soon, especially in matters like manners and sportsmanship. They think the 2-year-old should play politely months before he is ready to. They think a 3-year-old boy is a sissy because his best friend is a girl. They expect 5-year-olds to be good losers. But as the child grows older, he may progress more rapidly than the parents like. His natural assertion of independence and preference of friends to family may hurt feelings. Some parents who have loved the care and companionship of their baby try to prevent his attempts to break away. They rationalize their actions by saying, "He is not old enough yet."

Parents who know what to expect can avoid the vain and sometimes harmful effort to force a child beyond his years and can refrain when they feel inclined to interfere with normal progress. Unfortunately, individual differences are so great that no hard and fast timetable for social development can be constructed. Parents who take age norms literally can be disappointed and upset if their child either fails to develop according to schedule or fails to pass beyond a bad phase as soon as their baby bible says he should. On the other hand, parents should be on their guard against using the fact that individuals differ as an excuse for babying. The safe course is to give the child as much freedom as possible and to watch for his progress from phase to phase.

Expert opinion and common-sense observation agree that children do usually go through the following phases in the following order, if not at the exact ages indicated.

A. Dependence on mother. (0 – 18 months.) This is the time for fondling, cooing, and indiscriminate admiration from mother and father too.

B. Curiosity about other children. (18 months – 2 years.) This matches the child's curiosity about things. He tries to find out what other children are made of by pinching, pulling, hugging, etc. He'd throw them out of his pen if he could. At this stage let children try each other out, but don't expect them to play peacefully yet. Separate them before either has a chance to be hurt.

C. Parallel play. (2 – 3 years.) A child, when he first begins to be aware of other children as children, plays beside rather than with another child. When he approaches another, he grabs the other's toys, but hangs on to his own. He attacks without thought or animus. But the child enjoys and profits from occasional sessions with another. Play in the company of a slightly older, bigger child may be good for the 2½-year-old who is a persistent grabber. Parental admonishments do no good and punishment is a mistake. Play with the opposite sex is the same as play with the child's own sex.

D. Joint play. $(3-7^{\pm}.)$ Cooperation develops slowly. The child gradually learns to play with another child without fighting. He learns to take turns and to share. At first he plays best with one other child, and this may be true of unsupervised play up to the age of 6 or 7. Boys and girls play together. Parents should provide a safe place, simple safe equipment, and an alert ear or watchful eye. A child who continues to attack others may lack firm, consistent, affectionate discipline. The timid child should play with children who are his own size and no stronger, but shouldn't have his battles fought for him.

E. The "gang" and "best friend." (6 or 7 to $10^{\pm}$ in girls, to 12 or 13 in boys.) As the child breaks away from the family, he finds some of the security he needs in group membership and friendly loyalty. Fights and fighting are common even with best friends. Boys have fist fights and need to fight it out. Boys and girls at first play together, but soon group play is entirely separated by sexes. Friends and groups shift frequently. Competition between teams starts near the end of this period. A youngster wants privacy at home—a room of his own, possessions left as he left them, an inviolate diary (kept for all of two weeks!). This is a hard stage for parents to take, both because of the children's standards of dress, language, and behavior and because the parents are excluded from secrets, plans, and meetings. But strong efforts to restrict the child may estrange him. At least they will interfere with his trust in the family or with his loyalty to the group at a time when he needs both.

F. "Junior-high-school stage." (11 – 14.) This is sometimes called "pre-puberty," but girls may have begun to menstruate and boys to grow pubic hair. Girls are now ahead of boys in both physical and social development. Girls are usually first to want to look their best and to experiment with dating. Both girls and boys need the chance to experiment with more highly organized athletics and activities than the earlier "gangs" afforded, but are not quite ready for all-out competition. A well-planned junior high school becomes the center of life for children in this stage.

G. The teens. (12 – 17+.) Boys and girls begin to plan for adult life. They try to be the kind of people they would like to be and to prepare themselves for the kind of work they would like to do. Organized athletics give expression to the competitive spirit—actively for the participants and vicariously for the spectators. Coeducational activities like dramatics and the school paper permit cooperative effort at an almost adult level. Youngsters expect to be treated as adults and respond well if they are. Dating is a serious matter. Parents who have helped their children develop self-reliance, responsibility, and good taste in personal relations begin to reap great rewards.

Mistakes to Avoid

Our observation of Onlies who are having trouble in adjusting to school and in making friends suggests that there are some mistakes which their parents commonly make. The following rules of thumb will help you avoid these errors. They are particularly pertinent in the first years of school, but hold good in later years, too.

Don't overpraise minor achievements either in the home

or in play with friends. Sincere praise of a real accomplishment, of evidence of a desirable quality, e.g., courage, or of hard, prolonged effort, is all to the good. Thoughtless gushing makes a child expect other children to praise him for everything and interferes with the earning of real recognition.

Don't overdress a child or give him expensive presents. The Only is often the subject of jealousy on the part of other children because "he has everything." Observe your child's schoolmates and playmates and help him conform. The child who is not like others has an extra battle to fight.

Don't forbid any friendship. When you think a change is desirable (and it may be), provide new activities with different children and the child will shift of his own accord. Friends change very quickly, and a possible bad influence won't outweigh home training in the long run. Forcing a change may make the child resent you or deceive you and admire his friend even more.

Be ready to listen, but don't pry. Children do a great many things they never tell their parents. They are silent partly because they haven't time, partly because they like to feel independent, and partly, though rarely, because they are ashamed. Remember your own childhood! The parent who doesn't pry and doesn't ridicule or scold childish experiments has the best chance of being the child's confidant when the child needs to talk out his troubles. But if your child confides in the next-door neighbor, or a teacher, or an aunt or uncle, rather than in you, don't worry or pine. Such preference is usual and natural.

Set a good example in the number and type of friends you cultivate and in taking part in your community's life. Ward has shown a definite and significant correlation between lack of social contacts and community life on the parents' side and unpopularity and disturbing school behavior on the child's. If you have good friends it's easy to arrange for their children and yours to see each other—and their children are likely to be the kind you want your child to know. If you are known as an active, responsible, public-spirited person, adults and children will expect your child to be a nice person to know. He's sure of his original welcome, and that's more than half the battle.

Providing Playmates

In these days of small families, parents have to put a good deal of thought and effort into providing playmates for their child. The restrictions which heavy traffic put on the smaller child's free going and coming add to the problem.

One of our Onlies, for the sake of her Only, gave up a nice house in the country and moved into a suburban district where there are many large families living close together. The 6-year-old boy now has friends with whom he walks to and from school and who have the freedom of a series of yards for after-school play.

The mother of another Only, who lives in a more isolated section, speaks of herself jokingly as "the taxi driver." She says she spends her day driving—her husband to the train, her daughter to school, herself to market, her daughter from school to play with a friend, the daughter home, and her husband home from the station. We sympathize with her predicament, but we're confident that her efforts for her daughter will pay off.

One thing is sure. Propinquity is the major source of children's friendships as of adult romances. If a child is never thrown with other children, if boy never meets girl, mere willingness will do no good. The parents' role in the case of the majority of children is to provide the child with the opportunities for starting and for cultivating friendships. The child who has plenty of opportunities will almost surely make the most of them.

The outline of stages of social development which we gave

above will be a helpful guide to the parent in arranging playmates for a child. In the early months, the ordinary approach is to accompany another mother while pushing a carriage or to visit while sewing. Beginning when the children are about 2, mothers can take turns taking charge of two children. When this is going to be done, both the mothers should read and talk over this chapter, a book like Gesell's *Infant and Child in the Culture of Today,* and our *Better Home Discipline.* Advance thought about what may happen and advance agreement on techniques will prevent a great deal of unpleasantness between the children and between the parents.

From the age of 3+ to 6+, especially for those children who are not enrolled in a nursery school or kindergarten, there should be increasing experience with group play. This needs to be supervised (*not* directed), and again mothers can take turns. The groups should be kept small, four at 4 and never more than six. Two children play together better than three and, when numbers are even, the constant shiftings are not so likely to leave one child out. For the younger children, who still play beside rather than with each other, a sufficiency of play materials for each to have what the others have is desirable. (The Gesell volume has excellent lists of playthings and is filled with practical advice.) A sandbox big enough to hold several children at once is an invaluable resource. Outdoor play is easier to arrange than indoor. Periods should be short and not too frequent—an hour or less once or twice a week is a good start for 3- to 4-year-olds. The time can be increased as the children show they can manage the longer period. An age range of a year or more is helpful. Older children may volunteer to help with younger, and the younger learn from imitating the older. But bullies who always demand and get their own way should not be mixed with younger children—it's not good for either. Let convenience settle the proportion of

boys and girls, but try to include both. Do not expect or
suggest modesty in toileting. This is a good age for the Only
to learn the anatomical differences between the sexes.

Headquarters for the "Gang"

Once a child is in school, he has many automatic contacts. But through the elementary-school years he may need
considerable help in making arrangements for after-school
play. The great problem is space, indoors and out, and as
sports and games become the major interest, there is the
question of equipment.

Parents of an Only have both an opportunity and, perhaps, a mental hazard here. Their house and grounds are
likely to have more available space and certainly have fewer
groups competing for that space than in the case of larger
families. But parents of an Only, especially if they are getting on toward forty, are used to order and neatness and
nice belongings. They may dread the wear and tear on
property and on nerves that are inseparable from many running feet. They can make some compromises—e.g., insist
that the living room is theirs and that tag-players, hide-and-
seekers, railroad engineers, and mural painters confine
themselves to certain parts of the house. They can keep
their valuable china and antique furniture locked up, and
furnish the house with sturdy, or at least easily replaced,
china and furniture until their child is old enough to respect
and care for fine things. They can set up a few rules and get
agreement on these from their child and his friends. They
can send home (but welcome back next day) a child who
breaks an agreement. But no matter how reasonable the
youngsters are, they are not going to behave—and shouldn't
have to behave—like adults. The parents can comfort
themselves with the knowledge that nothing is so valuable
to a child as to feel free to bring his friends home. A popular, out-going, college-age Only says, "I never had any prob-

lem about friends. Our house was always the headquarters for the gang."

Parties

Parties are a help in establishing contacts for a child, but they are not without dangers. A young Only may look on a party as more evidence that everything is to be done to please him. His parents have always provided toys and catered to his wishes, and now they are providing live entertainment. The result may be an appalling exhibition of bossiness, conceit, and selfishness. Unfortunately the young guests are more than likely to kowtow to the king of the minute. They don't like him and may not want to come back. But for the present they follow the line laid down by their host, at least for a short distance. The result is an increase in the child's difficult tendencies, and in his unpopularity.

How wrong an Only's party can go is clear in a grandmother's account of one. "I had never dreamed that our Mary was so bossy, until her seventh birthday party. First, she told me what she wanted: her summer play-school group to lunch. They came, all dressed up in lovely little dresses and wash suits, duly bearing gifts. Mary ripped the wrappings off and squealed with delight. When we went into the dining room she announced: 'When I say sit, you sit, and when I say stand, you stand!' While I was starting to clean up after lunch, she mounted her new bike, and ordered her friends to follow her around the block. They did, straggling through traffic. I saw them from the window and ran out before anyone was killed. Then she chose the games and directed them and quit each as soon as she tired of it. One young guest was bright enough to phone his mother to come take him home. And I've told my daughter that next summer I think Mary had better go to camp."

Forewarned parents can reduce the chance that a party

will turn out this way by instructing the child in the duties of a good host. For example, they can point out that they themselves always serve a guest first. They can provide gifts and prizes for every child at the party and make their child wait his turn. They can take an active hand in the proceedings. A children's party is one time when parental domination may be justified.

Public Parks

Public parks and playgrounds are a boon to city dwellers. Older children can go by themselves and be sure of finding company there. Younger children can be taken and turned loose, while their parents sit on benches and watch the children's gyrations from a distance. Sunday afternoon is father's turn to act as guardian, and he may actually serve as goal-tender in an impromptu soccer game.

On a recent visit to Rio de Janeiro one of the authors stopped to watch children at play in a small park on Sunday afternoon. There was a good deal of simple equipment—ladders, slides, swings, and tunnels—with children swarming around now one piece and now another. Two obviously well-trained supervisors, a young man and a young woman, kept unobtrusive watch and occasionally suggested to a child that he wait his turn. Off in one corner a group of 6- and 7-year-olds were running around in their stocking feet (their Sunday shoes piled in a tangle on one side), chasing a small-sized soccer ball. A father kept goal at each end. Monday morning, a question to a guide about the park brought the statement, "I was there. Playing soccer. I always take Mike there on Sunday. It's safe." And it turned out that Mike, aged 6, is an Only.

Take Another Child Along

Excursions and travel offer the parents a chance to include a friend of an Only. The prolonged period of being together lets the caution (perhaps even the politeness) which characterizes brief encounters wear off. The common goal and shared experiences bring the children closer together. The added responsibility which the parents assume is somewhat balanced by the times when the children amuse themselves. The children, when they go back to school or to their neighborhood group, enjoy a certain distinction which is good for them. A father can take a child and a friend downtown to see a parade, to the park for a model-airplane meet, off for a day's fishing, and on a camping trip overnight or longer. We know one lonely Only who goes everywhere with her parents and never has a friend along. She's nervous, tense, finicky about food, and in general a pest. Another Only, also a girl, has had a friend on trips across the Continent and to Europe (the friend's family paid their share of expenses). This Only is relaxed, cheerful, popular, and a good sport. We can't help thinking that there is a connection between the experiences and the result.

Visiting

Visiting is an excellent means of throwing children together on an intimate footing that at least resembles family life. Visits can be for overnight, for several nights, or for fairly long periods. Some precautions are in order. The young child's first visit away from home is preferably made with his parents and to a relative. With that experience behind him he feels more confidence if he is left for a few extra days when his parents depart or if he goes all on his own. However, we have reports of children whose first overnight visits were to neighbors' children at the age of 6 and entirely successful. We also have reports of a 6-year-old being so overwhelmed by the strangeness of bed and room that he had to be bundled up and taken home. By 8 or 9 a boy or girl is usually able to spend several nights at a friend's or with relatives. If an Only is the small host, he can be made to realize ahead of time his duties in the way of yielding precedence, sharing, and cooperating. He can be told not to boast or blatantly exhibit his possessions. If the Only is going visiting, he can be prompted about voluntarily doing his share of what chores there are.

When an Only asks if he can have friends to visit, his parents should do their best to cooperate. One of our Onlies, now a young teacher, says that she grew up in a house by the shore, a half-hour's bus ride from the town where she went to school. This didn't seem very far to her parents and they had no idea how isolated she felt. They were surprised but agreeable when their 10-year-old daughter began to ask to have friends spend the night and the week end. The young friends, delighted by the beach and the country, were always glad to come. Naturally they returned the invitation. She had been conscious of being an Only and had longed for brothers and sisters. But the frequent visiting made her feel much better, and she is convinced that it made life easier for her in college and in her profession.

Camp

At any time from the age of 8 on, a boy or girl who doesn't have much opportunity to join in out-of-school group play will derive special benefit from going away to camp. We believe that camp is good for all children. It may be a very special experience for an Only. The life is intimate —four to six or more children to a tent or cabin—and the youngster has to learn both to get along with others and to be himself in the midst of others. He has the chance to learn to handle himself physically in individual and team sports. He has the security of a routine without the regimentation to which he is subject in school. He is away from his family and learns to care for himself socially and personally. At the same time he is safeguarded by a group of counselors whose job it is to see that each youngster profits as much as he can and as enjoyably as he can from his camping experience.

What a good camp can do is shown by the case of an Only whom we have been observing for several years. He is the son of a widow who has had to work to support him. He was somewhat overprotected as a child and had not learned to get on well with other children. He was timid. In matters like clothes and haircuts he showed the lack of a man with whom to identify. He was sent to camp for a series of summers, and year by year has made great strides to a stronger, better personality. He has learned to swim well, to play tennis, to play baseball. He's better about doing his share of the work whenever he is with a group. Going back to camp as an old boy, able to show the new boys the ropes, gave him more self-confidence. Now he is a senior aide in the camp and looks forward to being a counselor. The chances are that he will be a good one.

There is a great demand for good camps, but some which claim to be good are far otherwise. Parents should not take a catalogue at its face value but ought, if possible, to visit several camps the summer before they expect to send their child. If they think their child has any special problem, for example, that he needs experience in athletic competition, they should inquire how the camps have handled other children of the same type. A Federal pamphlet, *Your Child from 6 to 12,* which rates camping as highly as we do, gives the following points that parents should check either by a personal visit or by investigation of references. 1. Sanitary arrangements should be sanitary! 2. A health certificate should be required from each camper. There should be a resident nurse, and a doctor in residence or within easy call. 3. Is the milk pasteurized? Are the meals planned by a trained dietitian and prepared by skilled personnel who have health certificates? 4. Are swimming arrangements safe and are children always under observation when they are in the water? 5. Are the camp director and counselors well-trained, experienced, wholesome people? What opportunities do they have to spend their free time in wholesome ways? 6. Is there enough variety of projects and activities so that each child can enjoy himself? Is there plenty of lee-way for individual interests—not too much fixed routine? Is there planning for activities involving both large and small groups and some chance for a child to do things alone if he wants? 7. Is there too much emphasis on rewards, prizes, and competition? Do the children feel that they are always being compared with others, or do they feel, as they should, that they are judged by their own efforts and perseverance?

Going Away to School

Boarding school has the same advantages for an Only that a camp offers, but it is more expensive and exercises more influence on the youngster's future. Leaving out of account the merits of a private-school education compared with a public-school education (a question we have discussed at length, including methods of appraising public and private schools, in our book *Bright Children*), we feel that an Only might well be sent away to school if his parents have any feeling that they are dominating him.

One pertinent suggestion has been made by several of our Onlies: the Only who goes away to school or college should have roommates. One Only still regrets the fact that her family had arranged for her to room alone at college. She says, "If I had had roommates I'd have made more friends more quickly—to say nothing of knowing what was going on. Things happened right in my dormitory freshman year that I didn't know about until we'd graduated." A college junior says, "The hardest thing I had to do in school was to get used to roommates, but I'm glad my school didn't have single rooms. I'm still rooming with one of those I had my first year in school." The parent of an Only says her son is going to have a roommate, because "I learned more about how to adjust to other people, to live and let live, to share but to stand up for my rights, by rooming with three girls than I ever learned at home as one of four children."

The decision to send an Only away to school needs great courage on the parents' part, and greater courage may be needed to force him to stay in school if he is homesick (see Chapter XII). But the pain of parting can be looked on as a sacrifice made for the good of the child. The mother and the father of one of our Onlies found that they could not help making him the center of their lives and focusing an unhealthy amount of attention on him. When they realized that they couldn't control their feelings, that they were worrying over the child and spoiling him to his detriment, they sent him to a good pre-preparatory school, then to a prep school, and then to college. It was a heroic series of decisions to make but, judging from the results, it has paid big dividends. The boy came through World War II with honor and has made a good start in his profession. He's happily married and about to be a father. When he visits his parents, they still incline to fuss over him. He and they can now laugh at their telling a veteran to put on his rubbers, but they all know how bad the result might have been had he been subjected to that type of control all his life. As it is, the young man's war record, his happy marriage, and his good start in his chosen field of endeavor fill the parents' life with pride and joy.

The Scouts, the Y, and Other Clubs

There are a number of organized out-of-school activities which give youngsters aged 8 or 9 and older a chance to make friends and share group projects under favorable circumstances. The Scouts and the other clubs have a large accumulation of knowledge of worthwhile group activities.

The parent of an Only does well to encourage a boy to join the Cub Scouts and a girl the Brownies as soon as they are eligible. (We know a good mother who, finding that no Brownie group was available in her neighborhood when her only daughter reached the proper age, proceeded to organize one.) A little later, if the youngster wants to join a specialized group like the Sea Scouts, by all means let him.

The way an Only may profit from out-of-school clubs is shown by a brief autobiography of a candidate for admission to college. She writes: "In my early youth I was extremely shy and didn't outgrow this trait until, when I reached junior-high-school age, I joined the Order of the Rainbow, of which I am now an officer, and the Pilgrim Fellowship. I also joined the Y.W.C.A."

There is perhaps something in the question of one mother of a 10-year-old Only: "How much danger is there that the modern child will be overorganized—i.e., in too many activities such as school orchestra, church choir, Girl Scouts, etc. etc.?" We feel very strongly that growing children, and adults too, need a certain amount of time alone—to loaf, to think, to dream, to catch up with themselves. But this ability is promoted rather than handicapped by a reasonable amount of activity with organized groups and a large amount of association with friends. There's a great deal of difference between being lonely and being alone. The adult Only who has a compulsive need for company, who has to be going and doing every minute, is more often than not one who felt lonely as a child. Certainly the parent of an Only should take every chance to build up the child's opportunities to make friends.

Athletics

Again and again both men and women Onlies tell us that they wish they had had more rough-and-tumble play and had participated more in sports. They think, quite rightly, that children who grow up wrestling, climbing, running, and playing contact games like football with other children develop better, both physically and emotionally. The child who has this type of play acquires specific skills and also increases his strength, agility, and ability to coordinate. He learns endurance. He's not timid in a situation that involves physical effort and the chance of a fall.

Certainly athletic abilities—physical strength, the love of using it in a game, and specific skills—are an asset in making friends. Of course many Onlies have these abilities. Our case histories include the captain of an Ivy League basketball team and an All-American football tackle. But we see too many Onlies who, as Levy says, have had only "verbal, passive social experience in childhood" and, as van Krevelen says, "hang on the edge of the play-group, watching."

Several causes, individually or in combination, may explain an Only's comparative lack of rough-and-tumble experience. Brothers and sisters, and especially brothers, do fight a great deal. Parents, even those still young enough to enjoy a roughhouse, cannot offer a child the serious competition that siblings do. Parents, thinking of contact sports like football, see more of the disadvantages—the dirt, torn clothes, and possibly broken necks—than the advantages. They do not encourage, and may actually forbid, their child's participation. They may supervise a child so closely that even if he has many playmates he doesn't have the chance to wrestle on the living-room floor. When he goes to school he is so far behind the other children in physical experience and in skills that he is a handicap in games. He is not chosen, he takes refuge in reading and nonathletic recreations, and falls further and further behind his age mates.

Most children go through a period, sometime between 9 and 12, when physical combat is the preferred means of settling an argument. Some individuals, like the nations of the world up to date, never outgrow the inclination to fight. Now, few parents want a child to grow up to be a prize fighter and still less the kind of person who gets involved in brawls on the street or on the floor of the United States Senate. Most feel, and there are psychologists who agree with them, that if individuals could be trained not to resort to fighting, nations would not resort to war.

It seems to us a mistake to think that if children never fought, nations would never fight. Anyhow, we're quite sure that left to themselves children will fight, and that when a child is hit he ought to hit back. We would confine control to seeing that a child is not constantly bullied by an older, bigger child or a gang. Some good teachers, when well-matched boys fight, stop them just long enough to provide boxing gloves, and then see that rounds and rules are observed. Our own experience confirms that of generations of parents and teachers. Fist fights rarely result in bad injuries and still more rarely interfere with friendships. The habit of fighting is generally outgrown before the teens. Boys who have had their share of fighting are as likely as not to be polite, friendly young men with sympathy for the underdog.

Starting a Sport

What can parents do when they realize that a boy or girl in elementary school or later is not taking much or any part in games and athletics?

The first reply to that question is to say what shouldn't be done, and very definitely what fathers should guard against. There's a tendency for parents to blame the child's character, rather than his pre-school experiences or themselves for the way they have brought him up. They call a boy "Sissy"; they say, "You could if you only would"; and they shame him with remarks like "You throw like a girl." Ridicule and shame may kill any athletic ambition a child has.

Fathers are particularly likely to scorn a physically timid son. They decide to take him in hand and teach him to swim or play ball. They are impatient with his lack of ability, set too high standards for him, and scold the while they drive him to practice. They may succeed. We know one Only who was driven by his father through hours of practice at shooting baskets. He made school and college teams, but he has a distressing stutter that is quite possibly a direct result of the father's relentlessness.

Professional coaching is another matter. We have several cases where parents of Onlies, both boys and girls, have helped their children by enrolling them in "classes" organized by professional coaches. The parent that can afford professional lessons for a youngster may help him develop a series of skills that will be a lifelong asset, that will increase his fun in playing games and give him the knowledge necessary to watch games intelligently. Coaching is most readily available in sports like swimming, golf, and tennis. But there are camps and Y's that make a point of giving lessons at various levels in basketball and baseball. Teams are set up on the basis of ability, and as a child improves he can go up the ladder.

Sometimes the best way to start a boy or girl is to suggest a new sport and make it available. If a youngster shows an interest he ought to be helped as much as possible, certainly with suitable equipment and perhaps with lessons. An Only who was on his college swimming team writes: "I was the fat boy of the neighborhood. My close friends were the athletes, and I found no athletic knack until I found that swimming came more easily to me than to my leaner friends."

The classic sublimation for the boy who has not the physical equipment to make a team is for him to become its manager. The swimmer just quoted goes on to tell about his son, also an Only: "I was too fat but my son has always been thin. Like myself, he tried all sports with no great success. He did his best to make the swimming team at college, saw it was probably impossible, and became manager."

Managing the team is surely good for a young person's experience in group contacts and for his feeling of achievement. We are all for it. And we are great believers in young people becoming proficient in the sports which they can play all of their lives, e.g., tennis, golf, swimming, and bowling. But at the same time we feel that only children, both boys and girls, have a great deal to learn from team play in sports which involve both bodily contact (like football, soccer, and basketball for boys, field-hockey and basketball for girls) and strenuous competition. They deserve every opportunity and all the tactful encouragement which their parents can give them.

Dancing Classes

A child who has one or more siblings of the opposite sex has a double advantage in social relations. The child learns to get on with the other sex without thinking about it. The child has a chance to meet and associate very informally with the girls and boys who are friends of his sibling. A coeducational school helps the Only in these matters, but not enough. Classroom activities, particularly in the elementary school, are compartmentalized in the child's mind as *school* rather than social. Voluntary out-of-school activities during the elementary-school years are largely divided along sex lines. But formal dancing, with its emphasis on etiquette, accustoms boys and girls to regarding each other as partners. Boys may hate dancing lessons, but when they begin to go to dancing parties they will be in a strategic position. To dance well is almost the greatest social asset a teen-ager of either sex can have. In the meantime, a dancing class is an excellent means of giving children a chance to make new friends. A boy who objects may be won over by telling him that boxers dance to help their footwork.

Signs of Trouble

Here are some signs which appear when a growing child is not adjusting as well as he might. Alert parents can read these signs and redouble their efforts to help their children make friends.

Immaturity. Crying, fears, grabbing, tantrums, boasting, and self-centeredness are all typical of young children at certain stages. But the child who continues to behave in these ways when his contemporaries are outgrowing them needs help. First grade is perhaps the crucial period. The Only who has not had much chance to associate with other children before he enters Grade I may in the beginning behave in all of these ways, but he should outgrow them during the year. A first-grade teacher reports: "The five Onlies in my class of twenty-five children were all self-centered in the beginning of the year. Contact with the group of children helped them, and their personality development was marked by the end of the year."

Playing mainly with children of a different age or sex. The child who prefers to play with younger or weaker children may be overtimid and unwilling to compete with his peers. These are also characteristics of the boy who plays mainly with girls, and of the girl who plays mainly with boys because they grant her special privileges. Parents who are at a loss in their attempts to get their child to play with his peers should consult his teacher. Once aware of the problem, she can do much to give him good group experience in school.

Lack of a "best friend." A best friend, or rather a series of best friends, is practically a necessity in the development of good social relationships. Parents can help a child make such a friend by taking potential friends along with a child on excursions and trips, and by encouraging their child to join groups which center around some interest of his. He is quite likely to find some one child in the group who will be drawn to adventure with him in his hobby.

Unwillingness to participate in extracurricular activities in secondary school and college deprives many Onlies of one of the best sources of companionship and one of the best means of making lifelong friends. It is a point on which research agrees that Onlies as a group are weak. Onlies in secondary school are old enough to face this problem for themselves. They can consider their own interests and aptitudes and make an honest effort to participate in activities that they know they would like. If they have a sincere interest, success in making friends will ultimately follow.

No "girl friend" or "boy friend." Dating is a part of our American mores. We're sorry for the 16-year-old girl, an Only, who wrote, "My major problem is getting a boy friend. I get so tongue-tied that it is almost impossible to keep a boy interested." The remedy again is through groups. A girl who will join a high-school dramatics club or a hiking club may soon find a boy who takes the initiative. Being a good dancer is a help. Also, girls—and boys—need to be helped to look their best. Several studies have shown that popularity depends not so much on beauty as on vitality. Have the youngster go privately for a talk with a sympathetic family doctor about things like pimples and a vitamin-full diet.

Most Succeed

We started this chapter with statements from Onlies and parents of Onlies which showed how much importance they attach to good friendships and how difficult it may be to make these. The fact remains that our study of adult Onlies indicates that most of them have succeeded in finding good friends, in marrying, and in winning places for themselves in their communities. Friends are not everything—even our maladjusted Onlies are not friendless—but they are certainly a main resource in times of trouble and in times of pleasure.

IX.

The Calculated Risk

LIFE has always been hazardous and always will be. The person who avoided all risk could not stay alive; he would die from lack of movement if not from lack of nourishment. In the world today it is not really possible to avoid major dangers like crossing streets and traveling in automobiles. Onlies cannot be shielded from these dangers any more than non-Onlies. And some Onlies, whatever precautions their parents take, are going to be among those killed and maimed by accidents.

In the face of the inevitable, parents must take a calculated risk. A child who is granted independence runs some chance of being hurt or killed. If he is not hurt at all, or at least not seriously hurt, he will, by the exercise of responsibility, be learning to take care of himself and so reducing the chance of being injured or killed at some later time, perhaps the next day, perhaps in fifty years, when his parents are not present to control his actions. The parents must weigh the possible present danger against the probable reward of greater safety in the future.

Naturally parents wish to spare a child as much pain, physical and emotional, as they can. However, a great many parents, perhaps especially many parents of only children, go so far in their attempts to safeguard their children that they are constantly interfering with the children's efforts to plan and do for themselves. A child whose drive for independence is thus thwarted may find it hard to stand on his

119

own feet when parental support is eventually withdrawn, as in time it must be withdrawn. Personalitywise, such a child is like those Mandarin girls who were crippled for life by having their feet kept tightly bound through the years of growth.

Our materials indicate that the principal reason why parents of Onlies do not give their children more independence is their fear that the child will be accidentally killed or injured. Our case histories of adult Onlies are full of comments like: "My parents never let me have a bicycle"; "They never let me go out in a canoe"; "I was the last person in our crowd to drive a car." And our observation of the daily lives of only children and their parents convinces us that caution is often carried to the point where it defeats its own purpose.

It Would Not Have Happened If—

One of our most tragic cases of an Only is that of Mary. Until Mary was 8 and in the third grade her mother always drove her to and from school, although the school bus made a regular stop to pick up several children right across the street from Mary's house. Each schoolday from the time she started kindergarten, Mary looked with longing at the little knot of children waiting for the bus and sighed when she had to climb in her mother's car and be driven to school. She felt left out and peculiar, and she was always begging her mother to let her go with the other children. Finally her mother gave in and said that Monday morning Mary could go on the bus. The children gathered as usual. Mary, keyed to a high pitch of excitement by having at long last won permission to use the bus, kissed her mother good-by, and dashed down the porch steps and across the road right into the path of an automobile. She was killed instantly.

Mary's mother undoubtedly blames herself bitterly for giving Mary permission to take the bus that day. Other mothers may well consider the fact that thousands of children in kindergarten and first grade, including the great majority of Onlies, do take school busses or walk to school through city streets every day. They are as safe as can be because they were trained to take care of themselves and given responsibility for themselves. Children who are unduly protected are not permanently safe from accidents, as Mary's case shows. Moreover, they are exposed to personality damage. We have records of several Onlies who are transported by their parents to and from high school each day. These youngsters show definite signs of maladjustment.

Children Under Five

We are not advocating a policy of blind chance, of letting children do what they wish when they wish. Of course parents have an obligation to take all reasonable precautions to ensure a child's safety. Most particularly they must be vigilant to protect the child under 5.

The Metropolitan Life Insurance Company reports that there are 5,500 fatal accidents to young children annually in the United States and Canada. Accidents account for one fourth of all the deaths among children 1 to 4 years old in the two countries. Burns, drownings, falls, and poisons are great killers, but the automobile is the leading cause of fatal injuries—accounting for more than a third of the total. The deaths and injuries due to automobiles occur while children are playing in their own yards and driveways or are riding with their parents, as well as when they are playing in the street.

The great majority of accidental deaths of children under 5 could be avoided if parents exercised proper precautions. Experts on safety all agree that children under 5 cannot be trusted to keep themselves out of trouble. The small child's natural curiosity is rampant. He has to see, touch, taste, and manipulate. The scissors have two points, the electric outlet two holes; will the points fit into the holes? Explaining, reasoning, punishment, and painful experiences do not guarantee that a child will "play safe" in the first place or fail to repeat dangerous behavior. A young child is still so undeveloped mentally that he cannot be expected to understand or to remember what is dangerous. He may realize that something he has just done displeases his parents, and yet repeat himself a few minutes later. And the young child is so undeveloped physically that he cannot rescue himself when he is in difficulty.

The responsibility for the safety of the child under 5 is directly and indirectly the parents'. It cannot be shifted to the child himself. But this does not mean that the parents must watch the child's every move. This isn't good for either parents or child. They can make a careful survey of the place in which a child is to be left alone—the yard where his playpen stands, the screened porch, his own room—and remove the dangers.

All parents mean to keep matches and poisons locked up where a small child cannot get them. But many parents never think about a 2-year-old climbing out of a second-story window. They do not think when they leave a baby in his bath while they answer the phone that they may find him drowned when they return. An incredible number let crawling-age children play in the room with an oil burner that can be upset or a gas heater that can be turned on. These are some of the more common causes of death or injury in the home. There are too many more for us to consider them in detail here. Insurance agents are glad to provide pamphlets that will help parents locate dangers and correct them. But no matter how safe a room may be, there should always be a responsible person within sight or calling distance of any child under 5.

From 5 on, children are increasingly able to look out for themselves. They can understand and obey rules. (It's always wise to keep rules to the minimum essential for safety. Then they can be remembered, and enforced more easily.) Children aged 5 and older are less likely to repeat dangerous behavior which has caused them hurt or for which they have been punished. They may even stop to think and not do something which their parents would not approve. In truth, the well-trained child is often more cautious when alone than when with his parents. This is especially true in the case of traffic hazards. When a child is walking with a parent, both the child and approaching drivers relax and shift the responsibility to the parent. If the parent is not alert for the unexpected, tragedy may follow.

Readiness for Responsibility

Children differ greatly in the amount of responsibility which they can assume at a given age. No one should say, "A child of 5 is ready to cross the street alone," or, "A boy of 18 is ready to drive a car." But parents are able to form a pretty sound opinion of what their child can do with reasonable safety if they will gradually but steadily let him do more and more for himself and by himself. If the child is progressing, if he is being given the chance to take more and more responsibility for himself and showing that he can handle it successfully, the general rule is to let him do what others of his age are doing.

Reasonable Precautions

Of course all parents should try to see that their children do not take unreasonable chances. And all parents should try to see that their children are given the kind of training and equipment which minimize danger. Take, for example, the question of a boy's playing high-school football.

Rough-and-tumble sports are good experience for an Only, and football is the archetype of such sports. But high-school football results in more injuries than all other sports put together, and a few players are killed each year. The great majority of injuries and deaths are due to games played on stony fields, or without proper pads and head-guards, or by players who have not been taught to handle themselves skillfully. Parents should not let a boy play un-less a good field and good coaching are available. They should see to it that he has the proper clothes and equip-ment and, after talking over their reasons, ask him not to play without these. With proper safeguards, he should be allowed to go ahead. There is still a chance of his being in-jured or even killed, but hardly more than of his breaking his neck by slipping in the bathtub.

What holds true for football holds true also for a great many other sports and activities. From the point of view of danger, swimming is the most important. Drownings are a leading cause of accidental deaths of both children and adults. Forbidding a child to go in the water won't neces-sarily save him from drowning. He may disobey, or he may fall in. Rather than forbid him to swim, be sure that he learns how to swim well and that he understands the princi-pal hazards (e.g., heavy surf and striking a concealed rock while diving). It is entirely reasonable to ask him to agree not to swim alone. But it is not reasonable to ask him not to swim when swimming is one of the most popular American pastimes.

Some parents try to give their children the benefit of sports with other children but to protect them by being on hand to supervise. We think it significant that the children we know who have been treated this way are more or less maladjusted. And one of Levy's cases is a boy who at 16 had never been allowed to play any athletic game except base-ball, and that just when his mother was with him. Imagine what the other boys said and how the 16-year-old felt.

The Automobile

One of the decisions most parents face is when to allow a youngster to drive a car. Driving is dangerous at any age, and teen-age drivers, partly because of inexperience and partly because of temperament, are involved in more accidents per mile driven than any other age group.

We have several accounts of Onlies who have been involved in bad automobile accidents. Our cases are not numerous enough to afford any basis of comparison, so we cannot say whether Onlies are more likely to have accidents than non-Onlies. We should very much doubt that they are. But because money may be available and because parents may yield to the youngster's pleading, an Only may have a car of his own before most of his contemporaries.

One newspaper report tells of an Only, aged 18, who was driving home alone from a dance. A heavy rainstorm was in progress. He hit a tree and was found dead in the wreckage. Another newspaper report tells of a 17-year-old who was given a secondhand motorcycle. On his very first ride he dashed out of his driveway and was killed by a passing car. Accidents of these types may be unavoidable. There are certainly thousands like them each year which do not involve Onlies. But just as the parents of an Only should let him engage in the activities that his contemporaries do, so also they should initiate appropriate safeguards. Safety experts agree that it is best for youngsters to be taught to drive not by their parents but in a special course, preferably in school. No boy or girl should drive before the legal age or contrary to the laws governing special licenses for young people, e.g., the New York laws that do not permit drivers under 18 to drive at night or within New York City limits. A young driver needs lots of practice and should have it under supervision. A youngster who breaks regulations, either those imposed by the law or those set up by his parents, should be deprived of the right to drive. But boys and girls who are qualified for their licenses, who have shown skill in driving, and have proved that they can accept and exercise responsibility in other matters should not be kept from driving.

Worry

We spoke earlier of children whose parents worried unduly and who became worriers themselves. The parent who is always afraid that something is going to happen to a child —that he will catch a cold or have an accident—can't help showing his worry. Luckily, just as most mothers soon realize that all the bad things which the books mention do not happen to all babies, parents who let a child engage in the activities normal for his age soon learn that he doesn't kill himself. After all, the chance is very slight. Though more than 5000 children under 5 suffer fatal accidents each year, there are more than 10,000,000 who do not. The chance of any particular child being a victim is only 1 in 2000. The chance of a child whose parents take the precautions we have discussed being accidentally killed is infinitesimal.

Confining a child will not prevent worry any more than it will teach him to take care of himself. On the contrary, the only way to stop worrying is, within reason, to make a child responsible for his own actions. Once you find that you can trust him, your troubles are over.

X.

The Need for Independence

EVERY baby has a strong urge to try to do things for himself. Psychologists have various ways of describing this natural phenomenon. Some call it "the aggressive instinct," others "the need for new experiences," and others "the need for independence." The report of the Mid-Century White House Conference on Children and Youth, *Personality in the Making*, uses Dr. Erik Erikson's term "autonomy," the need to be an individual and act as one.

All psychologists agree that by his second year a baby is of his own accord trying to overcome the complete dependence on his mother which marks his first months. His mind, muscles, and coordination have developed to the point where he can move much more freely, and he seems eager to try out these new abilities.

If parents foster the child's explorations, if they stand aside and let him try for himself and praise him when he succeeds, he will continue to grow year by year in the ability to do things for himself and will gradually acquire the ability to see for himself what he should and should not do. By the late teens he achieves that responsible independence which is the characteristic of the truly mature person. Granted freedom to act, he tries to do what is best for everybody, for himself and for others, under the circumstances.

If during childhood the drive toward independence is thwarted, the individual remains socially immature and therefore unable to take the normal adult's care of his own

127

personal concerns. He is still less able to assume the normal adult's share of responsibility to the community.

Normal Progress

No matter how patient a parent is and no matter how willing he is to take a risk in letting a child do things, there is always the practical question: What actually should the child be able to do for himself? It's foolish to wait for a child to button himself up when he is physically incapable of buttoning buttons. It's unduly dangerous to let him play alone near the water when he cannot swim. It's a mistake to put him in a social situation where ignorance exposes him to ridicule.

Thanks to Gesell and his associates, thousands of American parents have a good practical knowledge of developmental psychology. They are familiar with the various stages through which a child progresses emotionally, mentally, and socially as well as physically. They know that the various aspects of development are interdependent. As the child's potentialities mature he utilizes them to express himself and to relate himself to others. There are ups and downs, spurts and retrogressions. But the overall progress along all lines is forward, and really amazing in its magnitude.

Parents of only children stand to profit in a particular way from Gesell's work because they lack the experience to tell them what to expect a child to do. *Infant and Child in the Culture of Today* and *The Child from Five to Ten* contain forty-two gradients. Parents can feel confident that they are not overprotecting a child who moves through the various stages described in these gradients.

Parents should always keep in mind Gesell's admonitions about ups and downs and about individual differences. You can't hold a stop watch on a child and at the second when he is 3 years old say, "Now unbutton your front buttons."

You can expect him to progress from undressing to dressing after a fair interval, but again there is nothing very definite, there is no set number of months. The rule is to let the child try each operation when he wishes, and when he proves he can carry one out to give just the minimum of assistance.

It's a lot easier and quicker for a mother to continue to undress and dress a child long after he has all of the abilities necessary to take off or put on his clothes than it is for her to leave these matters to him. And the mother may receive a deep emotional satisfaction from waiting on her child. But she is doing him a disservice by substituting the expectation of being waited on for the desire for independence. When a child is once so accustomed to service that he no longer wants to help himself he may never outgrow this babyish stage. He stops trying to do things for himself. As the psychiatrists say, he suffers from a fixation at a low level of emotional and social development. He remains immature.

All psychologists are now agreed that normal progress to independence proceeds best when a child is thoroughly convinced of his parents' loving support. This conviction can be firmly established in the first year, when the child is completely dependent on his mother for survival. This, according to *Personality in the Making*, is the first stage in personality development, the stage of trust which is a necessary precursor of the stage of autonomy.

The consciousness of loving support, the knowledge that in case one encounters difficulties beyond one's capacity one's parents will come to the rescue, is a continuing need throughout the period when independence is being established. The individual who is sure that his parents will uphold him has the confidence necessary to try his wings. Then, as he flies further and further by himself, his self-confidence grows.

Dangers in Dependence

We have already shown how difficult it is for the dependent only child to adjust to first grade and to learn to associate with other children. Luckily the aggressiveness natural to human beings makes such a child struggle to overcome his dependence. He generally succeeds during his elementary-school years, and, as a result, may have an easier time than his contemporaries, most of whom fight the main battle of their rebellion in the early teens. He has fought and won his fight. But some young people, both Onlies and non-Onlies, remain dependent. These have trouble in college and in later life.

Dr. Clements Fry, the chief psychiatrist of the Yale Department of University Health, in his book *Mental Health in College*, says that one of the major causes of the troubles of students who are referred to his office is a failure in establishing independence. Even among his patients from the graduate and professional schools, one third are still engaged in freeing themselves from restrictive family ties. Fry describes sixteen cases of overdependence, of whom five are Onlies.

A student who has not developed a measure of independence before he goes to college finds the change abrupt. He is inexperienced in organizing his time and in making decisions. He may have become so used to dependence that he does not wish to be independent or to find friends outside his family. He is timid and unable to stand competition. He is resentful at finding himself in difficulties. He may withdraw to the security of the family—actually leave college and go home. Or, Fry says, he "may assert his independence through symbolic action": defy the college authorities, ignore classes, play cards constantly, date girls every night, drink, run away, or even commit suicide.

Another psychiatrist, Dr. Erich Fromm, in his book *The Forgotten Language,* describes the case of an Only who as a child had been spoiled and waited on. He had not been allowed to swim or engage in other sports. He had sometimes wanted to rebel against restrictions, "but why complain when he had all these wonderful things: admiration, affectionate caresses, so many toys that he could throw them away, and almost complete protection from all outer dangers." As an adult he failed to use his brilliant mind to master anything, but instead tried to win easy praise. When not praised he became angry and cruel. He remained a child in his "grandiosity, dependence, fear and rage." He was cured only after a long period of psychiatric treatment.

Psychiatric literature cites many examples of the unfortunate results of overdependence in early life, and among them are many Onlies. Maladjustment in marriage, homosexuality, and breakdowns following the death of a parent are some of the more serious difficulties. Less serious, but still handicapping, is the inability to make a decision without seeking advice. Dependent people suffer from constant anxiety, and, as Dr. John Whiting says, are forced to ask help "not so much because they need it but because they find that the very act of dependence reduces their anxiety." These are the people who as children were not given independence and the responsibility for making their own decisions.

Signs of Overdependence

Just as independence is usually achieved gradually, so overdependence is the cumulative effect of many incidents. The parents rarely set out to keep their baby a baby. But —whether the reason is an unsatisfied psychological need of their own or fear for the child's safety or unthinkingly doing things for the child just because this is quicker and easier than to wait while he does them for himself—they so interfere with his natural progress in independence that they make dependence habitual.

We have already discussed Levy's four criteria of extreme overprotection: namely, excessive contact, infantilization, prevention of independent behavior, and control that is either excessively dominating or excessively permissive. Parents who go to extremes are probably unable to realize what they are doing. They need professional help. But many parents can recognize a tendency on their part to prevent or interfere with developing independence. They may realize, as they read what we have said about adjustment to school, about playmates and friends, and about taking calculated risks, that they are doing some things they should not do or at least not doing all that they should. Here are two more examples that show an unfortunate tendency to overprotection.

One mother took her 16-year-old boy to consult a friend of hers about getting a job for the summer. Every question the friend asked Tom the mother answered before Tom had a chance.

A 12-year-old girl attends a public school near her home. She is required to come straight home from school each day. In the summer her parents take her cruising with them. They do not invite other children to accompany them, though their boat sleeps six. Last summer they tied up at the dock of acquaintances. There were two boys in the family who were about the girl's age. Urged by their parents they asked her to go to the movies with them. She pleaded to be allowed to go and permission was granted. But her mother soon followed and sat in the back of the theater where she could keep an eye on the youngsters.

Generally the child's own behavior is the parents' first sign that they have not been encouraging independence and responsibility. The spoiled child is not a pleasant companion even for doting parents. If they continue to put up with him, the reactions of other children when he first goes to school may ring an alarm.

Even without much spoiling, an Only may become dependent on his mother for companionship. The young child who is *always* saying, "What shall we do now?" and, "Me, too," has not learned to play independently. The school-age child who shows no initiative in making friends, who comes straight home every day to be with his mother or to read by himself, is not developing sufficiently.

The Golden Mean

Helping a child become independent does not consist in abruptly shoving him out of the nest. We wish to emphasize this point very strongly. Some parents, after reading books and articles which show the evil results of continuing dependence, have taken sudden drastic action like leaving a child alone in the house all night when he has never been alone, or sending him on an errand to a big city when he has had no experience in finding his way, or shipping him off to boarding school without warning. All of these experiences can be taken in stride at the proper time by a person who has made the gradual progress that is normal. But *forcing* independence is like throwing a child into the water and saying, "Sink or swim." There's a great chance that he will sink. If he does survive, he may cease to look to his parents for help or advice of any kind.

We feel that parents can encourage independence without being harsh and without abrogating their rights. If the transition from the complete dependence of the newborn baby to the complete responsibility of the full-grown adult has been the slow, gradual affair that nature intended, the question of parental right will hardly arise. The parents will continue to carry out their duties, including that of sometimes saying, "No!"

Nor does the child in establishing his independence necessarily oppose his family or forsake his family ties, as some psychologists and sociologists seem to assume. In the first place, parents who have followed the steps which we discuss in the next two chapters normally take pride in their child's achievements. In the second place, an individual who is really responsible is the very one who considers the advice, feelings, and rights of others though he knows that the final decision is his own.

XI.

When Should Your Child Stay Alone?

PARENTS who leave a child all alone can be pretty sure that they are not overprotecting him. And a child who stays alone cheerfully has achieved a measure of independence.

These statements hold good over a wide range of ages though, of course, the length of time the child is alone and the circumstances under which he can be left alone vary with age. For example, it's a good sign when parents follow the advice of the baby bibles and let a child sleep in a room of his own. It's a good sign when a young child can amuse himself for considerable periods without crying for his mother. But the crucial test comes when the child is old enough to be left all alone at home in the evening while his parents are out about their own concerns. In other words, when can you dispense with a baby sitter?

Parents of Onlies sometimes feel that this is an especially difficult question for them to answer because they cannot apply the rule of thumb, "Treat your child the way his contemporaries are treated." They say that most of his contemporaries have siblings and that several children can be left together without a baby sitter earlier than one can be left alone. The children are company for each other and there is some safety in numbers. One might wake though the others slept in case of fire. If one became sick another could telephone for help. But eventually individuals are going to have to stay alone. At what age should they begin?

135

What safeguards can be set up? How should the child be prepared?

To help answer these questions we made a survey of one hundred families. We deliberately picked responsible families in good neighborhoods in a city, a suburb, and a semi-rural town. Most of these families live in single houses, but some live in apartments and some in two-family houses. The ages of the children living at home ranged from a few months to 18 years. There were 22 Onlies in the group, 9 girls and 13 boys. These ranged in age from 8 years to 12 years. All the families were asked if there was *always* someone at home when a child was at home at noon, in the afternoon after school, and in the evening after supper. They were asked if they had ever left a child all alone in the evening, without the company of either an adult or another child, and, if they had, at what age. If they had never left a child alone, at what age did they think they might? Finally they were requested to make comments and to offer suggestions.

Practically all of the parents gave us the same sound common-sense comment: "It depends." It depends on the child: his maturity, his experience, his age. But not so much on his age as you might think.

More than half of the families had left a child alone in the evening before the age of 12. Four fifths had done so before the children were 15, and all but one of the seven 16-year-olds had stayed alone.

Onlies had stayed alone earlier than children with siblings. Of the thirteen boys who were Onlies, five had first stayed alone at the age of 10, three at the age of 11, and one at the age of 12. One of four families who had never left a boy alone said they might when he was 14, and the other three said, "Never." Of the nine girls who were Onlies, one had been left at the age of 8, one at 10, and four at 11. Of the families of the remaining three girls, one said they might leave theirs at 14, one at 15, and one at 16. These replies show that Onlies can be left, and many are left, alone at relatively early ages.

It Depends on Temperament

The value of our survey rests not so much on this outcome as on the comments which the parents make. One mother reports that she and her husband leave their only daughter of 8 alone. "She doesn't mind. On the contrary, she's proud of her independence." A mother of 11-year-old twin boys says, "One twin can be left alone. The other—no. He's too insecure." Here are some other comments: "I don't believe in leaving any child alone" (only boy, age 11). "We started to leave our boy alone recently when he insisted he was quite happy with his dog" (only boy, 11). "Our daughter [an Only] baby-sits for pay at 11."

A Slow Start

Our hundred families agree wholeheartedly with our opinion that the development of independence should be a gradual matter. Their comments show that they have not made "staying alone" a matter for sudden and drastic action.

Security grows only with experience. A few minutes at a time may be enough to start staying alone. That way, the parents return before a child has a real chance to miss them, so that he has no occasion for panic and for feeling abandoned. Gradually, instead, he discovers for himself that there is nothing frightening about being alone. He begins on his own to develop a feeling of security and of self-sufficiency, by a process that can be as painless and slow as a well-managed weaning, and with results just as important to successful growing up.

Certainly everyone would agree that no child under 5 should be left for even a few minutes unless he is in a "child-proof" room or yard and has a responsible person within call. Some would say this rule should be observed through 6. But parents who report that their 11- and 12-year-olds seem happy alone, almost all say that from the age of 7 on their children were accustomed to being left alone for brief intervals, perhaps while their mothers chatted with a neighbor or posted a letter. Only gradually, as the children grew older and seemed ready for it, were those few minutes stretched to an hour or two.

A child can come home from school at noon and in the afternoon to an empty house at an earlier age than he can be left alone in the evening. Gesell says, and our parents agree, that most 9-year-olds are capable of being alone in the afternoon and of starting preparations for supper. We think, however, that the child should know in advance that there will be no one at home when he arrives. And it's better if the mother is at home most afternoons until the child's own activities begin to keep him away from home after school.

When you first begin to leave a child alone after supper, it is wise to keep the periods short and, even so, not to make them too frequent. Several parents make comments like, "We leave our 10-year-old for a half hour or an hour Friday nights when we go shopping." And a 10-year-old Only whom we consulted said he didn't mind being alone at night, "but an hour is long enough." Parents who say they leave 11- and 12-year-olds often add that they do this "very occasionally" or "never after ten-thirty." Eight-thirty was the latest for one 11-year-old.

Someone Near

Shortness of time away is the first step. Nearness should be a part of it, and continue even when the time lengthens. One couple with an only child reports: "In the summer we go next door to play bridge. When it begins to get dark our 11-year-old boy quits play and puts himself to bed. We're usually out on the neighbor's screened porch and he can see us and call to us."

Some parents use the telephone for close touch. Those who ask the child to do the phoning say it gives him a project that makes him feel self-sufficient and capable. If they are in the home of a friend he knows, he can picture the whole scene and feel a part of it, too.

Friendly neighbors, when houses are close enough together, are frequently called on to bolster a child's feeling of security (and his parents' peace of mind) by keeping an eye on his house and by being on call. One family has a fisherman's conch, on which the children, aged 13, 11, and 6, can sound a call to a relative who lives only a few hundred yards away. The children know it works because they tried it out to see. But they've never had to use it or the phone.

Inviting Other Children In

Parents differ very decidedly on whether it is better to leave a child all alone or to invite a neighbor's child to spend the night. Most of them like the idea of inviting another child in, because the children are company for one another. Others have tried this once and regretted it the same night; there was too much excitement, roughhousing, and damage. "Now we leave Mike, aged 11, alone," concludes one parent. But we have accounts of very successful "visits" at this age. When the children prove they can be responsible, the Only profits from the experience. We think it's worth a trial.

Fire—Accident—Burglars—Rape—Kidnaping—Sickness

Parents who are unwilling to leave a child of any age alone are generally afraid of what might happen to him if they did. This is an acute phase of the problem which we discussed in the chapter on calculated risks. All we can add to what we said there is that for years we have been collecting accounts of disasters which befall children. We do not have a single example of burglars, rape, kidnaping, or fatal sickness in the case of children left without baby sitters. Studies of rape, molestation by sex perverts, and kidnaping show that these are actually exceedingly rare, in spite of the news stories. When they do occur, the child is usually on the way to or from school. Burglars, according to the crime-prevention experts, are afraid to enter a house where lights indicate that anyone is present and able to use the telephone. A light in a bathroom is particularly discouraging.

No one is going to leave a sick child alone, whatever his age. Sudden sickness so severe as to prevent a child's telephoning for help is unlikely.

Accidents do happen, but they happen as often by day as by night. A boy who cannot be trusted with a chemistry set in the house at night shouldn't have a set at any time.

Fire is the big risk, but this is true when the parents are at home as well as when the children are alone. For three successive days, including the day when this is being written, our newspaper has carried accounts of children burned to death in house fires. In two cases, the parents were at home. In one case, five children, the two oldest 16 and 15, were at home alone. This was a "flash fire," and adults would have been as helpless as the 16-year-old. The problem is not one of leaving a child alone but of making your home fire-safe. Ask your insurance agent for help.

Precautions

In addition to making your home as fireproof and accident-proof as possible, there are certain other precautions that you should take when leaving a child alone.

Be sure that the child knows where you are and can reach you. Do not change your plans without letting him know. Do not get home later than you said you would unless you let him know.

Be sure that the child is competent in his use of the telephone. Have the numbers of your doctor, a neighbor, and the fire and police departments printed in big letters and numerals by the telephone. Clip to the list a special note with the number at which you can be reached.

Tell the child to leave lights lighted in the living room, the hall, and the bathroom. Plenty of light is a safeguard against accidents as well as against the slight risk of burglars.

Notify near neighbors that you are going out. Tell them where you can be reached and what time you expect to be back. Of course, when they go out you will return the favor.

Our parents are divided on whether a child alone in a house is safer asleep or awake. A mother writes, "I do not feel that a child should be left alone asleep. Even at 14 or 15 they sleep too soundly." Another says, "We leave our boys, who are 12 and 10, alone after dinner on their honor to go to bed at eight-thirty. This is the first year." We ourselves feel that if children are accustomed to getting themselves to bed there is no gain in telling them to stay up until the parents return or pledging them to go to bed at a particular time. The important thing is to take the precautions which we have mentioned.

The Child Who Is Afraid

There are adults who are afraid to be alone. Every creak is a stealthy footstep, boding no good. Every shadow is a lurking danger. Certainly you do not want to subject your child to unnecessary fear.

Psychologists differ as to whether fear of being alone is a basic fear which everyone has to learn to overcome or a learned fear. Some class fear of being alone, fear of the dark, and fear of falling as instinctual. John Dollard, of the Yale Institute of Human Relations, says that fear of being alone is not innate but is learned in babyhood. The baby, left alone, gets hungry and cries and cries. Finally someone comes and feeds him. He associates loneliness with hunger and discomfort, company with comfort. He may grow up subject to "compulsive sociability," the kind of person who can never bear being alone. Presumably a baby who is on a self-demand schedule will be less likely to develop fear and more likely to have a strong sense of trust on which to build self-confidence.

But if a 12-year-old is still afraid of being alone, the question of how he came to be afraid is pretty academic. There is nothing you can do about what happened to him before he was one! You have to begin, very slowly, to build up his self-confidence. You can leave him alone casually for a few minutes while you step next door. You can let him play or work alone on one floor while you are on another. You can assume that he will go upstairs to bed alone, putting on the lights on the way and leaving them on if he wishes. Do not ridicule him. Do not force him to stay alone for hours. If you have reason to believe he is afraid, do not let his first experience alone in the house last long, even if he insists that he wants to try it. When you do begin to leave him, be very sure that you return at the agreed hour, or he will worry himself into terror. Give him experience in being away from home. A boy who goes to camp and plays hare and hounds through the woods is too interested and excited to mind being alone. He unconsciously learns from the experience that being alone is not such a fearful matter after all.

Signs of Maturity

When our parents said that leaving a child alone depended not so much on the age as on his maturity, they added some useful comments on how they had decided that their children were mature enough. "The ability of the child to cope with situations" is the first criterion. They judge this by such things as how a child has reacted in the past when he cut a finger, or got sick, or they were unexpectedly too late to get his lunch in time for him to go back to school. One mother writes, "If the child has been taught to read and enjoy it, to use the phone intelligently, and to open a can and fix a meal, 12 seems a safe age to me."

Many parents first leave a child alone all evening when the child himself insists on it, like the boy who insisted he was quite happy alone with his dog. One 12-year-old also took the initiative one evening. He had chronic asthma, so his parents had been particularly reassured that his regular sitter was a retired trained nurse. But one night she couldn't come and they couldn't find anyone else. "Dad, did you have a sitter until you were twenty-one?" asked 12-year-old Jack. "But your asthma?" countered his dad. "I always start the croup kettle for myself," said the boy, "and I could ring the elevator bell or telephone you or the doctor." So they left him alone and have been doing so ever since. "He's really happier," reports his mother. And that's another test of when a child can be left alone.

The Benefits of Being Alone

The child who on occasion stays happily alone proves to himself and his parents his capacity for independence and responsibility. He gains in security because he learns that he is not afraid. And he has the opportunity to develop his own imagination and intellectual resources.

Ziman thinks that one of the advantages of being an Only

is that, because he lacks companionship, he has to learn to be independent and self-reliant. Dollard points out that the creative mind must be able to tolerate a certain amount of loneliness. Van Krevelen has listed a large number of creative geniuses who, like Robert Louis Stevenson, were only children. Dr. Alan Gregg, of the Rockefeller Foundation, points out that many creative men and women have had, like Stevenson, much "illness or loneliness or lots of time to swing on the gate" in childhood. So don't hesitate, when circumstances are right, to leave your child alone now and then. You will actually be helping him toward the self-reliance that brings security, and real enjoyment of his own company—a lifelong asset for anyone.

XII.

Fostering Independence and Responsibility

A CHILD has to be the father of his own independence. By the nature of the matter no one can be independent for him. But his parents have many opportunities to foster his independence, to let him plan and do for himself. There are many ways in which they can put him on his own where he has to be somewhat self-reliant. In the following pages we discuss some common parental attitudes and actions which help children develop wholesome independence and a sound sense of responsibility. We've tried to suggest some specific ways and means of helping a child, but in general all we can do is to emphasize the right attitudes and leave the details to you *and your child.*

Free Choice

Philosophers distinguish man from the animals by saying that man has free will. A man can deliberately choose what he wishes to do. Not all psychologists are as sure of free will as this. Human choices are to a considerable extent controlled by the way in which the individuals making the choices were brought up. But psychologists do know that a person who is lacking in the power of decision, who has trouble making up his mind when he is faced by simple choices, is not well adjusted to life. He's a man, but a weak man.

Power of decision comes from practice in deciding. A father of an Only says, "He hasn't learned to make decisions, not so much because he hasn't been allowed to but because, being with us so much, he hasn't had to." Parents know so much more than a child that the child, when he is with them, looks to them to say what to do and accepts their decision. But parents can leave many decisions to the child if they will deliberately plan matters that way.

One simple kind of choice to put up to a child is between two courses of action, either one of which is satisfactory to the parent: the kind of cereal to have for breakfast, which dress or suit to wear, to play in the bedroom or the kitchen. Trivial choices of this kind give the child experience, bolster his individuality, and make him feel adequate. They are good training for later, more difficult choices. And letting the young child choose is good training for the parent, too.

The next step is to let a child have his own way when what he wishes to do doesn't really matter. This gives him a chance to learn from his own successes and his own failures. Both success and failure are important in learning. We all tend to repeat what gives us pleasure and to avoid what gives us pain. If there is something we very much want to do and we fail in our first attempt, we avoid the method that failed and try another method. One sign of increasing mental and emotional maturity is the ability to foresee that some plans have a good chance of success and others of failure and to act accordingly. This ability comes partly from increased ability to think, but also partly from experience. If a child is to exercise forethought and so become responsible for his own actions, he needs experience in exercising initiative.

When we recommend letting a child learn by his own successes and failures we are not telling parents to permit their child to do anything and everything he wishes. Some rules and regulations are necessary for the child's physical and emotional safety. And the parents have a right to a measure of quiet and convenience. To achieve these ends the necessary minimum of regulations should be enforced consistently and firmly. As the White House report says, "Perhaps the most constructive rule a parent can follow is to forbid only what 'really matters,' and in such forbidding to be clear and consistent."

Play and Hobbies

Many benefits come to both parent and child from playing together and sharing hobbies, but a considerable amount of a child's play should be independent of both adults and other children. Free, unsupervised, uninterrupted play is the child's first and best chance to be on his own. And perhaps nothing is harder for the parents of an Only than to leave him alone to play: he is so much fun to play with and he enjoys playing with his parents so much! But see what happens. The parent piles up one block after another and achieves an Empire State Building. The child knocks it down, and the parent rebuilds it (we hope he doesn't say, "No! No!"). The child is fascinated by it, knocks it down, and asks to have it rebuilt. Everyone has a good time. But the child who is never allowed to play with his blocks alone is being robbed of exercise in his growing ability to pick up and let go of objects. He is getting the idea that he can't do things as well as his parents and so is developing a feeling of inadequacy. And he is learning to expect things to be done for him. If he were left to himself his tower would not have either the height or the form of the one his parent builds, but it would be his own. His success in adding one more block would teach him to try. The fall of his Leaning Tower would be a mild beneficial lesson in failure. When he learns by himself the advantages of a broader base for his tower he learns both to keep trying and to try new approaches.

Psychiatrists see other advantages in free play. Dr. D. W.

Winnicott advises parents of an Only to be sure that he has "much play alone with cheap toys *easily destroyed.*" Being alone and able to bang things about helps a child to work off anxieties and frustrations, just as his father feels better for a session chopping wood. The release the child experiences and the feeling of increased well-being that his father has are not signs of abnormality—quite the contrary! Play is good for everyone, not just for the maladjusted. All children, and especially the overneat Only, profit from the feel of mud, clay, sand, and finger paints, and from the chance to make designs with these materials and to build with blocks. The simpler the materials and the more they require imagination and initiative, the better.

An Only is particularly likely to be showered with expensive and complicated toys. He may possibly enjoy watching them operate when his father plays with them. But if they are too old for him, if he cannot use them one way or another for himself, he does not learn from them. A pressure-jet toy, the kind that needs a pump and water, is excellent for an 8-year-old but not even a matter of curiosity to the 5-year-old.

An older child should be encouraged to find his own interests and develop them into hobbies. The principle of free choice is important here. No one can say just what will spark a child's interest. Chance is a big factor, and so is the fashion of the moment among his friends. There is also a sort of age pattern; collecting usually precedes the use of tools. But why some people remain stamp collectors all their lives and others do not is a mystery. In any case, the parents' part is not to force a hobby on a child but to give him the chance to develop it for himself. All they need to do is to grant permission and to provide space, e.g., to let a child collect snakes and keep them in the cellar. They may help with some equipment, but even here the more the child does for himself, the better. Expensive equipment is to be avoided, because hobbies are likely to shift quickly, and parents who have invested heavily to help a child may try to make him keep at it.

Pets

A pet of his own is of particular value to an Only. The pet provides company and, if it's a dog, affection and admiration as well. The pet distracts some of the parents' attention from the child and gives the parents another outlet for pride and affection. The child has someone to talk to who won't answer back. He has a chance to boss instead of being bossed. Any pet can be a great builder of responsibility, if the child has the duties of feeding, cleaning (and cleaning up after), and nursing. Keeping a pet, especially a pair of pets, affords an object lesson in anatomy and a healthy means of sex education.

Several of our well-adjusted Onlies tell of receiving some or all of these benefits from owning a dog. But we know cases where the family has bought a pet for an Only just to satisfy the child's whim and then deprived the child of any possible benefits by taking all responsibility for the pet or by nagging the child about it. One mother of an Only unwittingly described the danger when she said, "John wants a kitten, but I won't let him have it. It would just mean that my father and mother, who live downstairs, would have to go up and down all day to take care of it."

The benefit in owning a pet depends, like everything else, on the attitude of the parents. They must be willing to let the pet be the child's, to leave all possible care to the child, and, if the child consistently neglects the care, to dispose of the pet.

Chores

Chores are frequently recommended as a means of teaching responsibility. It is said that the mere doing of a daily task day after day is in itself good for a child. We fully believe in the value of chores, but we must point out that the child who is regular and reliable in doing them is proving that he is responsible rather than learning responsibility! If chores are to teach a child initiative and responsibility, his parents must be very sure: (1) that the chore is a real contribution to the convenience, comfort, or finances of the family and not just a job imposed for character building; (2) that the child understands how the work he does makes a contribution; (3) that he receives recognition when he does a good job; and (4) that he is allowed some leeway as to time and method. It's even a good idea to say what things need doing and give him a choice.

It may be harder to meet these stipulations in the case of an Only than when there are several children in a family. There is less to be done and the mother, if she doesn't have an outside job, has more time to do it. Under these circumstances, two solutions suggest themselves. One is to adopt a family project like turning a basement into a playroom and let each agree on what he will do to help. The second possibility is for the family to take camping vacations together and so put themselves in a situation where everyone has to do his share.

Chores done as chores and household tasks undertaken as training are slightly different. Most girls and boys can be made to see the value in knowing how to cook and to keep house, and they are glad to have the chance to learn. They don't want to be like the man whose wife said, "Jack can't even boil an egg for himself. He never had to learn how because he was an Only." Moreover, learning to cook and to clean is good fun if the parent helps the child see why he should learn and, during the process, gives him the chance to act for himself.

Errands and Shopping

Errands and shopping afford excellent training in responsiblity. An errand makes a child feel he is doing something to help the family. It takes him away from the house and puts him on his own. It requires the exercise of responsibility and may require discretion. If it involves the expenditure of money and the exercise of choice, as in the case of shopping, responsibility is enhanced. The task can be fitted to the age and the experience of the child. The 6-year-old can take the next-door neighbor a recipe for which she has asked. A 16-year-old can go downtown and buy his own clothes.

How early a parent should expect a child to do errands which take him any distance from home depends on the child. One study of boys who showed eagerness to succeed discovered that their mothers had expected them to find their own way around town before they were 8. We know a 9-year-old who takes a bus to a town ten miles away to do errands for his mother. He carries her charge plate and is able to decide whether what a store offers is what his mother would like or not. The one time he was unable to complete the errand was when he was asked to exchange a girdle. He couldn't explain to the saleswoman just what was wrong!

As in all matters involving independence and responsibility, it is best to work up the scale gradually. First the child goes with his mother, then to the corner store alone, then downtown in his home town, and then to the city. The process may stretch out from the age of 5 to that of 12 or later.

Parents sometimes ask if a child who does an errand should be given money to spend for himself, a *pourboire* for a Coke. We don't think it makes much difference, provided he is always made to feel that what he has done has been a help. Certainly the chance to spend a nickel and no questions asked is good experience.

Allowances and Budgeting

Having the spending of an allowance is good experience in independence. Wise spending is a proof of responsibility. Allowances are now an almost universal custom, but parents always face the questions "How soon?" and "How much?" It's easier to answer the first than the second. Five is not too early to start giving a child a few pennies a week and letting him spend them in his own way, particularly if the other 5-year-olds in the neighborhood also have allowances. He can't hurt himself much. He may lose them even before he spends them, but that can be a good lesson, too.

The older the child, of course, the larger his allowance can be. For the Only it is important to keep his spending money down to the average of the allowances given his friends. Parents with an only child usually can afford to give a larger allowance than can their neighbors with several children. But our materials show that one of the handicaps an Only often faces is jealousy from children who have less. A big allowance can be a factor in this.

Once an allowance is started, the parents should leave the spending of it to the child. They can well say what they won't buy for him, perhaps ice-cream cones, candy, and hobby supplies, but they should not say what he is to buy or how he is to spend it. To give a child twenty-five cents a week and tell him he must put a dime in the church collection each Sunday both defeats the purpose of an allowance and encourages a falsification of accounts.

As a youngster proves that he can budget and spend his allowance wisely, the amount can be increased and the list of things the parents will stop providing lengthened. By the time boys and girls go off to college at 17 or 18 they ought to be having the independent spending of considerable amounts of money. A University of Pennsylvania survey of 600 boys and girls in junior high school disclosed that the majority are given much responsibility in buying clothes, making gifts, and accumulating savings. We know many 16-year-olds who are planning their own wardrobes and making all the purchases themselves. We know 18-year-olds who have saved enough money to buy and operate a car. However much money a youngster has, the parents should continue to be responsible for doctors' bills and medical expenses. Otherwise the youngster might slight his health. And the parents of a youngster who has a car should be sure that it is adequately insured to protect him and themselves. They are legally responsible.

One Only who read these paragraphs wrote in the margin of the typescript: "A girl feels very independent and grown-up when she is allowed to select the clothes she wants to buy." And that is just the point.

Earning Money

Money earned by working for other people is far more important in a youngster's mind than any amount which his parents may give him for doing chores or as an allowance. The University of Pennsylvania survey mentioned above and a similar one conducted by the University of Connecticut concluded that "money which these boys and girls earn themselves seems to have a higher priority and to give them a greater sense of personal freedom and recognition" than allowances, even when they are fully responsible for budgeting and spending.

Earning money is an adult occupation and so a symbol of independence. Moreover our society looks on earning with an approval that is freely expressed. A boy who can point to a car and say, "I earned and saved all it cost," speaks with justifiable pride.

These satisfactions, the feelings of independence and of

being recognized as an "up and coming" somebody, are valuable to an Only. So, too, is the knowledge, while he is on a job, that he must fulfill certain standards of promptness, regularity, and quality of work if he is to earn his pay. Some of our best-adjusted adult Onlies say they regularly earned money during their teens. One says, "I worked regularly every summer from the time I was 14. It wasn't consciously planned by my parents; it was just what my friends were doing."

The jobs open to young people are unfortunately limited in kind and in number. Parents of an Only do well not to limit them further by any false pride. Boys can mow lawns, run errands, wash cars, deliver newspapers, and, by the time they are in high school, help out in stores after school and baby-sit. Girls do most of their earning by baby-sitting, but we have records of a few girls who give piano lessons and several who work in summer camps and hotels. A considerable number make good wages by doing housework after school. One Only we know got a good start on funds for college in this way. In a servantless world, doing housework is a noble function and not beneath anybody. A girl who does it may learn more than she is willing to learn at home, and earn the while.

Baby-sitting has one special advantage for both boys and girls who are Onlies, that of giving them responsibility for young children and so preparing them somewhat to be parents.

Two words of warning are in order here. Paid employment should not be out of line with the youngster's age and strength. And the youngster should always have lots of time left for study and play.

Adult Guests

As the child's independence increases, his contacts with the world outside the family broaden. He meets people with habits and beliefs which differ from his parents'. He has to learn tolerance. There has been so much joking about the way teen-agers look down on their parents and think their parents' ways old-fashioned that the difficulties of the earlier stage, the stage of recognizing that the ways of one's parents are not necessarily either universal or perfect, have largely been ignored.

The Only, both because of his close association with his parents and because he lacks the standard of comparison which the behavior of siblings affords, may have an extremely narrow point of view. He may either keep this and grow up narrow-minded, or he may react violently against what he comes to consider his parents' narrow-mindedness. One factor in avoiding these extremes and helping the child gradually learn to respect both outsiders and parents, is for the parents to entertain adult guests informally in a manner that lets the child observe them and listen to them. The child then sees that his parents respect different points of view, and he learns not only what these points of view are but also politeness and respect.

"The Role of the Guest: A Study in Child Development" is the title of an article by James Bossard and Eleanor Boll in the *American Sociological Review*. The study is based on 200 autobiographies. It shows that in 115 cases the individuals described the visits of guests in terms that left no doubt how much influence on the child's development the guests had exercised. In general the guests afforded the child a standard of measuring his parents and his family's status, extended his horizon of beliefs and customs, taught him certain rules of social behavior, disclosed the possibility of inconsistency between adults' principles and practices (e.g., the white lie), and proved an intellectual stimulus. Sometimes guests produced conflicts and tensions in the family, but they often served "to unite the family in a mild conspiracy and so to heighten solidarity."

Visiting

One major means of achieving psychological separation
is actual physical separation in space. If parents arrange for
young children to be away from home on occasion and encourage older youngsters to go off on their own, the new
experiences, the new interests, the new personalities which
the children encounter *apart from their parents* serve to
make them psychologically independent. Levy found that
actual separation was about the most effective treatment in
cases of overprotection.

When parents plan wisely, the process of accustoming a
child to separation is neither abrupt nor dangerous, but
gradual and pleasant. We have already discussed sending
a child to camp or boarding school and letting him visit
friends. We are now coming back to visiting, because we
wish to emphasize its role in developing independence.

A visit away from home and parents is a major experience
in freedom. Our case histories show that many parents, fearing that they may dominate an only child, deliberately send
the child off on visits at a very early age. One mother says,
"My mother always dominated me and I determined to give
my daughter freedom. Beginning when she was 2 I used to
send her to her grandmother's for a week or two at a time.
She soon learned to look forward to the visits, and this convinced me that I wasn't essential."

Bossard ("Process in Social Weaning," in *Parent and
Child*) points out that visiting influences development in
most of the ways that having guests does. In addition, it
gives the child a feeling of achievement, a sense of freedom, and new experiences. It usually makes a child appre-
ciate his own home and parents more. There are some
dangers, including spoiling by "that most solicitous parent
in the world, a maiden aunt." Some people remember being
disillusioned by being exposed to experiences as varied as

sex play, having to use an outhouse, seeing meat eaten on Friday, and seeing adults get mad at each other. Some visits to relatives meant hearing constant criticism of the other side of the family. But in general, even when there were shocking incidents, visiting served a valuable purpose in social weaning.

Bossard found, and our case histories confirm his results, that visits may start at any time from the age of 2 to the age of 9. Early visits are usually to relatives, and overnight visits to friends come later. Of all the people Bossard studied, one in six did no visiting as children. The parents of this minority were fearful and dominating. The individuals who were not allowed to visit resented their parents' control at the time and in retrospect. Bossard concludes his chapter by saying, "The processes of growing up, becoming a person, being weaned from the parents consist of a continuing accumulation of the minutiae of experience in living. Visiting away from home involves some of the child's first social steps."

Travel

Visits and getting to and from camp, school, or college generally involve travel. Parents who can bring themselves to let a child do this traveling alone or with one or two contemporaries enhance the novelty and excitement of the trip immeasurably. The feeling of accomplishment which independent travel gives is a mighty bulwark of self-confidence for the child. And the fact that he has traveled alone makes him important in his friends' eyes.

The prospect of travel, especially when it involves changing trains, spending a night on a train or in a hotel, or finding the way through or about a strange city, gives pause to parents and child alike. We have for years been collecting data on children traveling alone, and have acquired some epic accounts of voyages by the very young. We have no instance of a child's being lost, or robbed, or raped, or kidnaped, or suffering any of the dire misfortunes which parents fear when a child sets out on a journey. Even loss of money or tickets is rare. The truth is that children who start out alone are usually determined to be careful and cautious. Conductors, porters, taxi drivers, airplane stewardesses, Travelers Aid representatives, are all interested in the young traveler and go out of their way to be helpful. Adults on trains and boats are friendly. One 7-year-old went alone by Pullman from Cleveland to New York. He was seen aboard the train, put in the conductor's care, and given just enough money to pay for his meals and tip the porter. When his father met the train the next day, several of the passengers said, "What a boy you have!" Inquiry of the boy about finances revealed that he had more money on arrival home than when he left Cleveland. Had he tipped the porter? Yes. What had he had for dinner? Quite a meal. For breakfast? Ditto. Then, whence the cash? "Oh, one man took me to dinner, and another to breakfast, and four gave me fifty cents each."

Another 7-year-old Only flew from Beirut to New York in the nominal charge of a woman passenger. He popped off the plane at Idlewild as cheerfully nonchalant as the most seasoned traveler. "I'd like to thank Mrs. Williams," said his grandmother. "Oh, she had a close connection to make and got off the plane first."

Despite such favorable experiences and the lack of disaster, we feel that learning to travel ought to be a gradual process like any other approach to independence. One good preparation is to have the child share in the planning of trips he is to take with his parents and, when he is on trips with them, to buy some of the tickets, order and pay for meals, and give tips. (The last is hard for some children to do.) He thus becomes accustomed to handling money and to the procedures involved in ordering and paying. He should have a definite sum of money to spend for himself and for gifts to his friends, and if he dissipates it all on the first day, he should go without for the rest of the time. The first trip alone may well be one that he has made before with his parents or other adults. A trip that involves a change of trains or crossing a city can be simplified by instructing him to secure porters and take a taxi.

Whatever the preparation, the first overnight trip alone is sure to be an exciting adventure. Apprehension is natural, but the successful outcome is sweet in proportion.

Homesickness

Our case histories of Onlies include a number of accounts of homesickness among children on visits or at camp, school, or college. In most cases the child is homesick during his first prolonged absence from home and not thereafter. In a few cases individuals who went away to camp without being homesick were homesick in school or college. There seem to be more girls than boys who are homesick.

A badly homesick child is a pitiful creature. Not even his nonhomesick friends can continue to laugh at him. He suffers from nausea, indigestion, loss of appetite, and sleeplessness. He has severe headaches. He is given to weeping spells. He is at once fearful and resentful. He's unwilling to engage in any activities. He refuses comforting of any kind. He besieges his family with letters, telegrams, and phone calls begging to be taken home.

Several psychological influences may combine to cause homesickness. The child, off in new surroundings, is deprived of the support of his normal routine. If the new situation is both strange and difficult, the child may "run away" in his thoughts and do nothing but think of that safe, happy place, home. The child may fear that his parents have sent him away because they do not love him, that he has, in effect, been abandoned. In his anxiety he may revert to infantile forms of behavior like crying and tantrums when he is awake and wetting his bed when he is asleep. It's as though he felt, "If I behave like a baby they will treat me like a baby and take care of me again."

One of our Onlies, now a happy, popular senior in college, told us, "I had never spent a night away from my parents until I went to school when I was 14. The nearest I'd come was when I was 8 and they took me to visit friends in New York and left me in the evening with the friends' children and their nurse while they went to the opera. Even then I was unhappy and felt sick. At school I was horribly homesick and unhappy. I think the fact that I'd been getting all A's in public school without much work and was getting very low marks in boarding school added to my discouragement. I begged to be taken home. My parents refused to let me come home, but came to see me twice in the fall and promised it would be better after Christmas. It was. I suspect that trying out for basketball and making the team saved me."

Time to get used to the new surroundings is the great cure, but there are some other things which help. The camp or school can try to interest the child in some objective that can be quickly achieved, like a better record this week than last in a routine task such as making up one's bunk. The child should be given a chance to continue any interest or hobby he may have had at home. Leaders among the other children should be prompted to choose the child for participation in their activities and to praise anything he does reasonably well. As recovery progresses, more distant, more difficult goals should be set, and sincere effort to achieve them should be recognized.

In the meantime, parents should be firm about not allowing the child to abandon school or camp, but do all they can to reassure him of their love. Some wise headmasters feel that parents should not come to visit a homesick child nor allow the child to visit them. Several cases make us question the wisdom of being too rigid in these matters. We have accounts of many complete recoveries that followed week-end visits home. The child may talk about a school more cheerfully at home than he feels about it when in attendance. He discovers that attending boarding school makes him somebody in his friends' eyes. He may find home is not the perfect place of his imaginings. And he goes back to familiar surroundings, rested and fed and ready to try again. We know one case where there was no change for the better until the family said that if the child would stick it out at school the first term he could stay home the second. The parents think that the child felt he had been sent to school because they did not want him, and that he recovered when he was given evidence that this was not so. But to let a child give up and return home permanently is probably not a wise course. If his homesickness is due to a tendency to withdraw from difficult situations, permitting him to withdraw confirms him in a bad habit. The girl who is allowed to abandon school because she is homesick may very well be the one who "runs home to mother" instead of trying hard to make her marriage work. We'd suggest, rather, that the parents be firm in stating that the child must remain in the camp or school, but at the same time plan with him something that they and he can do together during the next vacation. If either parent was ever homesick, the child can be helped by being told the circumstances of onset and recovery. Just knowing that one's parents know how one feels is a comfort.

The Parent–Teen-Ager Community Council

We have already discussed the great merits of a family council. The youngster who is given a regular share in planning family activities and in discussing family problems is receiving excellent training in responsibility. In families where the council is a habit, a youngster regularly brings forward his own proposals, asks for comment on his own plans, and is encouraged to speak for himself. The parents respect his opinions. He knows that he will be allowed to go ahead with any plan that is reasonable, and so he is not afraid to tell his parents what he hopes to do and to ask for their advice. All of which represents the very best in independence and responsibility.

In the last few years the family-council idea has become the pattern for community parent–teen-ager councils. Representatives of boys and girls in a given age range meet with representatives of their parents. The joint council discusses the activities which the teen-agers wish to undertake. Both parents and teen-agers express their opinions freely—and both are generally surprised at how closely agreed they are. Differences are ironed out, usually by compromise. If the community is a large one, a pamphlet may be printed and distributed to all concerned. This sets forth the standards of behavior agreed on by the council and serves as a guide to both parents and young people. Young people abide by the rules because they helped to make them. Parents have a ready argument against unreasonable plans, and do not have to wonder whether a youngster is right when he says, "All the other kids do."

Here are some agreements reached in successfully functioning councils.

Parents and students in twelve public, private, and parochial high schools in the Philadelphia area have agreed on midnight as a deadline for dates, except that "formals" may continue to 1 A.M. and home parties to 12:30 A.M. The hours for junior-high-school students are: dating 10:30, home parties 11, formals 11:30. The parents and teen-agers agreed that there should always be a common understanding of where and with whom the time is to be spent, and when the youngsters are to reach home. It's the boy's responsibility to make sure that his girl's parents, the girl, and he agree on these points.

The Mt. Vernon, New York, council has agreed on standards for hours and for such matters as allowances, drinking, smoking, driving, and party manners. The teen-agers on the council convinced the parents that teen-age drinking is not the problem that some newspaper stories suggest. The teen-agers recommended that no alcoholic beverages of any kind be served at social functions and that there be no smoking by high-school students. One of the council's recommendations indicates that not all parents are always perfect. Parents, the council says, should be willing to remain home when their children are entertaining, but "should not mingle with the guests."

A Westchester County council includes teachers as well as parents and students. In addition to dating, party hours, and party behavior, the council has considered "respect for persons and property."

As we said earlier, the teens are the period when young people are making their major effort to be independent. Therefore it is during the teens that young people face the greatest number of problems and the strongest feelings of doubt. They need the support of their parents, but this must be given in such a way as not to make the youngsters feel as dependent as ever. The rules arrived at by free discussion in a council are a perfect answer.

XIII.

Special Situations

THERE is overwhelming evidence that a child has the best chance of growing up to be a healthy happy person when he enjoys the care of a father and mother who love each other and love him. The evidence is equally strong that when a child loses either parent by death or divorce or when he grows up in a home torn by emotional strain, he suffers a handicap.

These adverse situations are not irremediable. It is true that a surprising number of delinquents and of emotionally unstable children come from broken homes. It is also true that large numbers of children from broken homes overcome their handicaps and grow up well-adjusted citizens. The number of those who suffer no permanent damage could be greatly increased if more of the adults in whose charge they are left understood the problems involved and took wise countermeasures.

Children of Divorce

The child of divorce is exposed to a twofold danger. First he spends some time, perhaps years, living in an atmosphere clouded by troubles. Then, already worried and upset, he is parted from one or both of his parents.

Some of our unhappiest Onlies are children of divorced parents. There is the little girl who is afraid of other children; she manages to miss the school bus by hiding just before it is due, and when her mother takes her to school, the child stands in the corridor outside her classroom and weeps

164

bitterly. There's the overserious little boy who lives with his mother and grandmother; money is so scarce that his birthday treat was to take one friend to the corner drugstore for a soda. There was the young man, brought up by his mother, who ran away from college and turned up in his father's office; the father persuaded him to return to college, and he committed suicide.

The tragedy is that parents who are unhappily married make life difficult for a child whether or not they get divorced. Parents who stay together for the sake of the child may think that they can conceal their differences, but they can't. The child senses that something is wrong, and the more mystified he is the more he worries. He may grow up a tense, insecure person. Dr. J. Louise Despert, in her penetrating book *Children of Divorce*, says that, though in her work she has never seen a seriously disturbed child whose parents were "happy, well-integrated partners in a harmonious marriage," she has seen many whose parents were unhappy but with no thought of divorce. Divorced parents may actually be better for a child than parents who live together in hate.

Parents who are contemplating divorce ought to plan together for the future of their child. They should remember that he is very much in need of security and of continuing love. He should be told what the plans for his future are. He should understand very thoroughly that he will not be abandoned. A passionate promise is not nearly as good in this respect as factual knowledge of where and with whom he is to live. The more continuity there is in matters of residence and routine, the more secure he will feel. Possessions of his own that he can take with him if he has to move are a comfort to him. Frequent moves, from home, to grandparents, to Reno, and to a new home can be very unsettling.

Regardless of custom, consideration should be given to whether or not the mother is the best custodian. If there is evidence of rejection, the child may receive a stronger, more abiding love if he lives with his father or grandparents or with foster parents.

Whoever has the care of the child after divorce should constantly strive to give him a sense of being loved and safe. Moreover, the child, lacking at least one parent of his own, needs to know adults of both sexes whom he can admire and love. He also needs many warm friends of his own age.

One of the recognized dangers when a child spends part of his time with one parent and part with the other is that the parents will become rivals for his affection. The parents may shower the child with attention and gifts, trying to buy his affection. The parent in charge of the child at the moment may belittle the other parent and, by diminishing the child's faith in that parent, undermine his security. An only child suffers grievously in this situation. He is exposed to the full force of each parent's bitterness. He may cease to love both parents, but work them against each other for what he can get out of them.

Some of our Onlies whose parents have been divorced have grown up to be fine people, happily married and parents of happy children. Despert, though her work as a child psychiatrist centers on emotionally disturbed children, is far from believing that divorce is a hopeless handicap to a child. As she says, "The child's need for help begins when the trouble begins," and if the parents will begin to help the child "as soon as they are aware of trouble in themselves, they will be rewarded by seeing the child grow in strength to deal with the trouble."

When One Parent Dies

Among our Onlies are 28 who, when still children, lost either father or mother. Of the surviving parents, 18 were widows and 10 widowers. All except one of the widowers, but only four of the widows, remarried. These figures are in line with those given by the United States Census Bureau for the population as a whole: wives tend to outlive husbands; widowers remarry more frequently than widows. The principal problem, both in frequency and in severity, seems to be that of the widowed mother who overprotects her only son. A boy needs a man on whom to model himself. Three of our cases from widely separated localities and quite varied backgrounds are pitifully alike. In each case the boy is exceedingly timid, has few friends of either sex, and in matters of clothing and grooming shows the lack of masculine influence in the home. These boys all attend public schools and are taught exclusively by women. None of them belongs to the Scouts. They are growing up in a feminine world.

When a widow has to work to support herself and her child, the difficulties are compounded. One of our adult Onlies, a woman, remembers that she was left all day in the charge of two teen-age girl neighbors, just out of school. The girls spoiled her badly. Her mother, conscious of how little she did for her daughter in the daytime, insisted on waiting on her hand and foot as soon as she got home from work. The Only feels that she has suffered all her life from having been so spoiled as a child.

Relatives can be a great boon to the child who has lost a parent. We have case histories which show the benefits of living in the house with an uncle, living with grandparents, prolonged visits to grandparents and to aunts and uncles, and living near "a raft of cousins about my age." Two of our widows have helped their sons noticeably by sending them to boys' camps for the summer.

The Stepparent

Stepparents can be the saving of a child, and they can be an unmitigated disaster. Because men are more likely to

remarry than women, and because stepmothers associate
more with the child, more women than men face this problem.

The stepmother who fancies herself in the role of mother
and sees all the things that can be done for "that poor
orphan" may be in for a rude awakening. The child has
probably idealized his own mother and thinks no substitute
good enough. Also, the child may have become used to having his father all to himself and resent bitterly the sudden
necessity of sharing attention and affection. The very things
the stepmother has looked forward to improving—the kind
of food the child eats, the clothes he wears, the hours he
keeps—may be established as pleasant habits. The demand
that they be changed fulfills the child's worst forebodings.

The bride stepping into this situation is more than likely
to be tense and anxious, too. The myth of the wicked stepmother (like that of the spoiled only child) puts the individual on the defensive. Fresh from the romance of
courtship and honeymoon, she may be altogether unprepared
for the devotion of the father to the child, and may be jealous of the child.

Three of our adult Onlies are still bitter against long-
dead stepparents. Two are men who had stepmothers, one
a woman with a stepfather. It happens that in each case the
child was sent away to school soon after the parent's remarriage. They still feel that they were treated cruelly. Two
of our adult women Onlies, whose fathers remarried and
then died, are still caring for stepmothers whom they dislike.

But we have cases where the adjustment to a stepparent
has been easy and pleasant. And there has been some research that shows how far from hopeless the problem is. Dr.
Janet Pfleger made an intensive study of 27 stepchildren
among the patients of a child-guidance clinic. She found
that 11 of the 27 had a positive good feeling for the step-

parent and the other 16 had mixed feelings. She felt that with care there was no necessity for lasting conflict. Certainly, if matters are managed rightly, the stepchild and the stepparent both stand to gain a wealth of love and security.

One of our happiest stepchildren is an Only who is the stepdaughter of an Only. The stepmother was the close friend of the child's own mother. The own mother died in childbirth. The father and stepmother married quite soon. The father says, "I think she married me to get the baby."

When a child is older at the time of the remarriage, it behooves the stepparent to move very slowly. One successful stepmother says of her step-Only: "My husband suggested that she call me 'Mother.' I vetoed that. I knew how she longed for her own mother. She suggested that she call me 'Aunty' and I agreed, but with a mental reservation. I treated her like a young acquaintance whom I wanted very much to have as a good friend. Little by little she learned to like me, and now we love each other. Now she calls me by my first name."

A gradual approach like this is the key to the stepchild's affections and so the means of giving the child the love he needs. The new stepparent should, of course, be eager to love and care for the child. In addition, it is wise to be prepared to ignore all sorts of shortcomings, and to capitalize on chances to do things for and with the child which the child enjoys. Then, if the elders set a good example, the child will outgrow his bad habits and grow strong in his good ones.

Grandparents

Our case histories present grandparents in three roles: as foster parents bringing up a grandchild who has lost one or both of his own parents; as members of a three-generation household; and as beloved hosts to young visitors.

Grandparents who have the sole responsibility for a child

can do a very good piece of work. If they love the child and the child loves them, they can really give him about as much as his own parents could. In some cases, particularly where the child's own parents have been divorced, there is a decided chance that the grandparents can offer him the best home he could find. The most evident difficulty is that of age. In two of our cases, grandparents caring for an Only died while the child was still young and left him orphaned for the second time. This contingency should certainly be borne in mind, and provision made for a guardian.

Grandparents with the care of a young child may, like overage parents, be set in their ways. They may expect too much in the way of decorum and manners. The efficient countermeasure is to provide the child with plenty of playmates of his own age and to encourage the child to make his house headquarters for his gang.

When three generations dwell in one household, the greatest problem is apt to be a disagreement over discipline. The single solution is for the grandparents to keep hands off. If the grandparent can learn to wait until he is asked for advice, he can be a fountain of healing wisdom. The child will gain security from the extra love he receives. He may even take the grandparent as a model for manners.

Several of our Onlies recall visits to grandparents as among the most pleasant experiences of their lives. One says, "They bought an old farmhouse in the deep country where all the grandchildren could come and visit. I spent my summers there with a horde of cousins. At home I was never allowed to do anything the other children did. In the country, I ran free—and how I loved it."

Another Only, now himself a grandfather several times over, says: "I was being made into a regular little Lord Fauntleroy—curls and all. I went to my grandfather and told him how I hated looking like a girl. He marched me to the barber's. That was a turning point in my life." Sometimes interference is justified!

The Adopted Child

The percentage of Onlies among adopted children is probably far higher than among own children. For example, an analysis of the vital statistics of Vassar graduates from 1900 through 1920 shows that 66 childless couples adopted children. Thirty-two of these couples adopted 1 child, 25 adopted 2, 8 adopted 3, and 1 adopted 4. That is, almost 50 per cent of these couples limited themselves to an Only, whereas about sixteen per cent of all married Vassar graduates of these classes who have children have only one child.

The dangers of overprotection, spoiling, and forcing are increased in the case of an Only who is adopted. The adoptive parents may feel a special obligation to prove themselves good parents and so overdo matters. Because they feel they owe the child every advantage, they may push him too hard. They may, for example, think of a college education as an advantage they can give him which he would not have had if they had not adopted him, and force him to go to college when he is not interested in that type of education and has not the ability to profit from it.

Parents of any Only are likely to worry about the child's abilities and about whether or not they are doing what is best for him. This tendency may be increased in the case of an adopted Only. Whenever anything, no matter how trivial, goes wrong, the parents wonder if there is some fault in the child's heredity or in their methods. They may be on the defensive and too quick to reproach themselves when they read or hear about methods of child rearing which differ from those which they have been using. They may think the neighbors are watching their every move and expecting the worst of the child and of them.

If the adoptive parents have failed to let a child know that he is adopted, they are tense for fear he will discover that he is not their own child. The child will sense this tenseness. When he discovers that he is adopted, as he inevitably will, he will add their worry to his own. He will imagine that his foster parents are hiding all kinds of awful things about his own parents.

When the adoptive parents from the very beginning treat the fact of adoption frankly and simply, they actually increase the child's security. He gradually learns that he was chosen because he was really wanted. One adopted girl in her teens told her mother, "I think being adopted is perfect. Do you suppose when I'm married, if I don't have children, they'll let me adopt a daughter?"

Luckily most adoptive parents, like most natural parents, quickly overcome their worries. They see their child progressing and developing, and they can regard the occasional difficulty in its true light as a minor episode in life. Adoptive parents who are inclined to remain critical of themselves ought to associate with other parents as much as possible. Listening to what happens to others' children and to what other parents do will reassure the adoptive parents very quickly. They learn that their child is not different from other children and that they are not different from other parents. They can give free rein to their love, and "love is enough."

Childless couples who are pondering adopting a child may ask two questions pertinent to Onliness. If they adopt a child, are they then likely to have one of their own, and if they do how will they feel about it? When adopting one child, should they plan to adopt two?

The figures seem to indicate that adopting a baby does have a favorable effect on fertility. In one study of 273 cases of adoption by childless couples, 200 of the women had a child within three and one-half years. In some of these cases the women had been hoping in vain for a child for ten years or more. Of course, they might have conceived anyway, but it is at least possible that the increased physical well-being that accompanied the emotional satisfaction of having a baby in the family resulted in pregnancy. All the evidence is that when pregnancy follows adoption the parents are equally fond of both children. The adopted child has already won their hearts, and if they have any feeling that the second baby was due to having adopted the first, they are grateful.

Though adopted Onlies do very well, we have no doubt that it is better for all concerned if two or more children are adopted. The dangers of overprotection and spoiling and undue worry are reduced. Adopted children growing up together have all the feelings and advantages (and the fights and jealousies) of true siblings. And there is much wisdom in the remarks of Jack Benny when he was asked about his adopted only daughter's getting engaged. According to the Associated Press dispatch, he said: "Well, you hate to see 'em grow up. But we've never interfered with her life. She's almost 20, she's old enough." Then he looked around his formal living room, and said, "I wish we had two more children hanging around. This is an awfully big house for just the two of us. Maybe we'll move to a smaller one."

It is not always easy to secure two babies for adoption, because the demand is about ten times the supply. The best chance of securing two or more babies, and certainly the best procedure, is to go to a state-approved agency and discuss the possibilities.

There are more older children waiting to be adopted. The adjustments involved for both the child and the parents are more difficult than in the case of young babies. The older child up for adoption may have been through a difficult time. Perhaps he has lost one or both parents, or perhaps his parents have proved so neglectful or evil that a

court has had to take the child away from them. The child
may have spent some time in a series of institutions or foster
homes. He may have developed bad habits. He may be
grieving, resentful, or suspicious. But couples who are willing to take such children into their homes and treat them
with patient affection often win loving loyalty in return.
The rewards are great. Anna Perrott Rose's book about
fostering older children, *Room for One More,* is moving and
authoritative.

In any case, all adoptions ought to be made through reliable agencies licensed by the state. The good agency is able
to assure the parents that the baby who will be their own is
physically and mentally all right. The agency's experts can
guarantee that there will be no conflict with the child's
natural parents. They can match the baby to the adoptive
parents' race, religion, and even intelligence. They arrange
a trial period so that if it looks as though legal adoption
would not be best for all concerned a halt can be called in
time. Very few children placed on trial by an agency are
not adopted, because such great care is exercised in the
first place.

Adopting two or more children and having own children after an adoption are both very different from adopting a child when there is already an Only in the family. In
this case the parents must ask themselves whether they are
adopting a child because they sincerely want children or
because they want their Only to have company. Adopting
a child as a playmate for an Only may be just another item
in the process of giving the Only everything he wants. In
one case, parents adopted a 4-year-old boy because their
6-year-old daughter kept begging for a younger brother.
The inevitable difficulties between two young children
started. The parents always supported their own child and
blamed their foster child. He withdrew more and more and

had to be committed to an institution. There have been so many disastrous cases of this kind that agencies are especially careful when they face a request for adoption from parents of an only child. This extra care makes the services of an agency all the more valuable in this situation.

The Physically or Mentally Handicapped Only

Parents who have a handicapped child may be unwilling to have a second. They may fear, especially in the case of feeble-minded or physically deformed children, that the second child will be like the first. The great expense of raising a handicapped child either at home or in a special private school may make them feel they cannot afford a second. In one of the best private schools for children suffering from cerebral palsy, one third of the children are only children.

The probability of a second child suffering from the same handicap as the first can best be estimated by a competent authority familiar with all the circumstances. First-born children are more likely than later-born to suffer from difficulties due to abnormal pregnancies and instrumental deliveries. Certainly a great many younger siblings of mentally deficient and physically handicapped children of some types are normal in every way. Parents who are in doubt about a second child should consult their family doctor and ask him where they can obtain expert advice.

Parents of a handicapped Only are generally most eager to do everything they can for their child. The formation of groups of parents who have children with particular disabilities has given many parents and their children new hope. These organizations promote special facilities for the care of handicapped children. They encourage research. They keep their members aware of new treatments and improved methods of care. If you have a handicapped child be sure to seek out and join with other parents who have children like yours. Your school superintendent can tell you what groups are already organized in your community.

Overprotection is especially hard to avoid in the case of a child suffering from any physical handicap. The parents are sorry for the child. They blame themselves. They feel they must guard him against ridicule, against letting other children see his deformities. The result may be that they hide the child away and keep him from developing as well as he might. As a matter of fact, young children are very casual about physical abnormalities. They may be unthinking and make remarks that seem cruel. Then, if a child is already sensitive about anything, whether this be a club foot or red hair, he will suffer. But if his parents have taken care to emphasize how he is like other children and to encourage him to play with other children, he and the others soon accept his limitations as natural. Of course a very lame child cannot play football. There are cases where a child has the best chance of development if he associates mainly with other handicapped children. But whatever the situation, the wise course is to emphasize what he has in common with normal children and to minimize his difficulties.

In the case of the mentally handicapped child, much depends on the degree of retardation. The somewhat slow child can profit from going to a regular school if his parents and teachers are understanding and do not push him too hard. A child who is more severely handicapped should be in a special class. The decision should be based on expert psychological advice. The parents will want to be sure that the advice they secure is the best obtainable. When they are, they should accept it. There are tragic cases of parents taking a child from one doctor to another, perhaps from one quack to another, and using up all of their resources in a vain hunt for help.

When an expert tells the parents that a mentally handicapped child should be placed in an institution, they may find his advice very hard to take, even though they recognize his experience and skill. To the parents, the child is their child, and no less so because he is handicapped. But they must try to look ahead to the time when he will be physically an adult but mentally unable to cope with life even in their home. And what will happen to him when they die? Eventually institutionalization will be necessary, and the experience of thousands upon thousands of families shows that it should be arranged early. If you are facing this problem we can't urge you too strongly to find the best institution you can and place your child's name on the waiting list.

A young couple that we know have a feeble-minded child. The father recognized the situation before the mother did. He and an understanding doctor gently persuaded the mother to arrange to place the child in a good state institution, where he will have excellent care and all the training possible. She cannot have another child because it was necessary for her to have a hysterectomy soon after the birth of the first. Now she and her husband have adopted a baby, and the agency has promised them another for next year. Our friends' lives have been tinged by tragedy, but they are happy loving parents, too. They know all that parenthood can mean.

XIV.

Vocational Success and Failure

OUR case histories of Onlies include two college presidents, several top executives of industrial corporations and banks, and many outstanding professional men and women: college professors, doctors, dentists, lawyers, scientists, and writers. There are very few of our Onlies whose careers can be classified as failures. This picture is much brighter than the gloomy one drawn by the pens of some psychiatrists and sociologists.

What the Pessimists Say

In the course of our reading we have compiled quite a collection of derogatory remarks about Onlies as workers. Here is a composite essay on the faults of Onlies, put together from the words of other writers. "The only child remains a spoiled child. When he goes to work he treats his employer like a parent. He expects to be indulged and protected. If he does not have his own way, he believes he is persecuted and usually resigns. He is hypercritical of everything anyone else does, and thinks he knows better than the boss. He has no initiative. He gives up the minute anything proves difficult. He is typically an occupational drifter, changing from job to job and ending up unemployed and unemployable."

Psychiatrists who describe Onlies, as a group, in these terms must, we think, be making a false generalization from their clinical experience. They have Onlies like this among their patients. They find that these individuals have been spoiled or overprotected or have unresolved Oedipus complexes. They think these difficulties are universal among Onlies and, therefore, that most Onlies are "unemployed and unemployable." But we are willing to guarantee that if they would make a fair study of their acquaintances they would find, as we have, that Onlies are on the average very much like non-Onlies.

We do not mean that we think overprotection and spoiling and misguided affection are not handicaps to vocational development. Levy's follow-up of his cases of severe maternal overprotection shows that most of them were poor employment risks. Two of his 5 Onlies who were old enough to work when the follow-up was made were evidently occupational drifters. But so were some of his non-Onlies. And it must be remembered that both the Onlies and non-Onlies in Levy's group were selected from patients at a clinic.

How Our Men Onlies Rate

Of our 75 men Onlies aged 30 or more (including a few now retired or dead), 15 have attained real distinction in their chosen fields. Four fifths, including the top 15, have earned more than adequate livings. These men represent a wide variety of backgrounds and occupations. In the case of each individual, his vocational success has been at least as good as one would expect for a man of his ability and background, and many of these individuals have done very well indeed. We do not say, or think, that they have done better than non-Onlies with the same qualifications but we feel sure they have done as well.

Six of our 75 Onlies have been vocational failures: 2 committed suicide while unemployed; 1, a heavy drinker, absconded; 1, a drifter and drinker, is unemployed and living with his mother; 1 changes jobs every few months; 1, after a long series of jobs, is now unemployed, but he has inherited enough money to live on in comfort and he makes himself useful in volunteer work. Of the remaining 9 cases among the 15 whom we rate as the bottom fifth, 1 has never worked because of tuberculosis, though he often talks of getting a job, and 8 have steady jobs, though the jobs do not seem to us to give full scope to their abilities. However, each of them has either inherited or earned enough money to live on.

The case histories of this lowest 15 show different combinations of adverse influences. Among those most frequently found are divorced parents, overage parents, ill health, and "too much money." We mention the last because, though a few of our small group of Onlies from wealthy families have been successful and even distinguished, an undue proportion of the wealthy group have poor vocational ratings. We'll come back to this later.

We have obtained additional evidence about the vocational success of Onlies by making a comparison of the careers of Onlies and non-Onlies in the Yale class of 1919. Of the 34 Onlies in the class, 29 served with the armed forces in the first World War. This is a larger proportion than that of the class as a whole. Twenty-one Onlies (62 per cent) won commissions as against 60 per cent of the rest of the class. Three won decorations for bravery in action. Of the 34, 28 (82 per cent) received the B.A. degree (as against 66 per cent of the rest of the class) and no less than 14 (41 per cent) received additional academic and scientific degrees as against 30 per cent of the rest of the class. By 1946, 5 of the 28 Onlies who were still living were distinguished in their fields, 19 others clearly successful, 2 were "underemployed," 1 was unemployed, and 1 was hospitalized. Compared with the class as a whole the Onlies' war records, graduate degrees, and business careers rank favorably.

The Women's Careers

Women's vocational success is harder to rate because of the large number who are full-time housewives. Of our women Onlies, 52 were actively employed when we obtained their case histories. Of these 52, 6 have distinguished themselves: a writer, a newspaper editor, a lawyer, an artist, a singer, and a psychologist. We have rated the other 46 as average or above in success. Not one of our whole group of women Onlies who wanted to work was unemployed, but 2 who had stopped work (to nurse sick parents) later took positions which did not let them use their abilities to the full.

The pattern of employment in the group of 127 Mount Holyoke women Onlies whom we studied is very similar to that of all Mount Holyoke graduates. In both groups, the majority are housewives, and of those who are employed, the greatest number are in teaching, the next greatest engaged in other professions, and the next in secretarial or clerical work. Proportionately more Onlies than non-Onlies are engaged in religious work and fewer in business, but the percentages for these occupations are low for both Onlies and non-Onlies.

It seems evident from these figures that, by and large, women Onlies, like men Onlies, are vocationally at least as successful as non-Onlies.

The Matter of Money

Parents of an only child have more money to spend on him than they would if they were forced to allot their resources among several children. This can be either an advantage or a disadvantage. It's an advantage when the money is wisely spent on education and training in line with the child's abilities. The large number of our Yale Onlies who took advanced degrees may reflect their parents' ability to support them during continued study. All of these men seem to have profited from their higher education.

Money is a disadvantage when the possessor, misled by its glitter, sets a false standard. Some parents, just because they feel they can afford the expense, force a child into situations which he has neither the experience nor the ability to handle. They make him take courses in school which are too difficult for him. They insist that he go to college though he is not qualified. They start him in a business which they think suitable though he has no interest in it. They bring him up believing that much of the work of the world is beneath him, is to be done by others for him at his pleasure.

Wrong attitudes toward money, rather than the actual amount of the family income, are what handicap a child. The case histories of our Onlies who seem to have been hurt by money follow a rather definite pattern. There was no need for the boys to do chores to help the family, and they didn't. They grew up being waited upon. They were allowed to spend considerable amounts of money before they proved themselves responsible. In school, though they were generally bright, they had both scholastic and disciplinary difficulties. When they did not get on well in one school they were promptly removed and sent to another. Their families expected them to go to the "best" schools and colleges, and, if the boys didn't work hard enough to get in, sent them to tutoring schools.

It may be a fine distinction, but it seems to us that these boys were not so much spoiled and overprotected as they were indulged at the wrong time. Most of them, for example, were subject to a certain amount of discipline and they were not allowed to have everything they wanted. But they were given presents, such as expensive cars, which were not suitable for their age. More important, when they had failed, as they did in school, their parents did not let them suffer the consequences. Their mistakes as well as their pleasures were treated indulgently.

Relatively poor parents who are determined to give everything to their child and to do everything for him can handicap him in the same way. Our two unemployed drifters both came from families of small means.

Domination

Money is not the sole root of evil. Again and again as we study our case histories we are struck with the way some parents have imposed their plans on a child more or less regardless of the child's own interests and special aptitudes. Fry does not exaggerate when he describes parents who select the clothes a boy wears, the friends he makes, the career he follows, and the girl he marries.

We know one Only whose father dominated every step of his son's career until the son was in his forties. The father, a banker, started his boy in real estate, put up the capital, and continued through the years to dictate policy and operations. The results, financially speaking, were excellent, but the son hated the idea that he could never act independently. Finally an Army friend offered him a position in a building-and-loan association in a city in another state. Our Only accepted over the bitter opposition of his father. Recently this Only's mother told us, "Ed has changed a great deal since he went to the Midwest. He seems a lot happier. He has more self-confidence. You know, it seems to me he even stands up straighter since he's been on his own."

In Father's Footsteps

Some parents are so afraid that they will be unduly dominating that they do not give a youngster all the advice they might. This is never so true as when a father bends over backward to keep from forcing his son into his business or

profession. There is, of course, a danger that a father may
bring cruel pressure on an only boy to "carry on." But a
father who is determined not to do this need not worry
about talking to his son about his work and giving him
every chance to help in any way possible. In fact, we know
no better way for a boy to find out that he does not like a
given kind of work than to hear all about it and take some
part in it. If he finds he does like it, he has a real head start.
A considerable number of our successful, vocationally well-
adjusted Onlies, including three of our four doctors, are following in their fathers' footsteps.

Vocational Guidance

The common safeguard against all of the dangers we
have been discussing is to help the child discover his own
major interests and to appraise his abilities and aptitudes.
If he knows what he wants to do and has the ability to do
it, the parents can go all out to give him the best possible
training and start. But discovering interests and appraising
abilities are not always easy matters.

For forty years and more, psychologists have been working on methods which would let them give sound vocational
advice. They have developed excellent means of discern-
ment, but they still have no magic eye. They cannot say to
one youngster, "You ought to be a doctor," and to another,
"You ought to be a banker." They can, however, say, "You
have [*or* have not] the kinds of abilities which people have
who are successful in such-and-such types of work. You
ought to choose a field of work in line with what you can
do." A very simple example is that of the boy who thinks he
wants to be a mechanical engineer. If tests disclose that he
has low mathematical ability but excellent verbal ability,
he will probably be wise not to go into engineering but to
select an occupation where mathematics is not so important
as the ability to speak and write well.

A bright person may have an embarrassment of riches when it comes to choosing a profession. A counselor can be of service here, both by helping the individual explore his own interests and by showing him the variety of occupations open to him. One of our Onlies was a good artist. After she graduated from college she set up a studio, but soon found that she was not really enjoying her work. She went to the guidance clinic at her former university and took a series of tests. The counselor showed her that her verbal ability, like her artistic talent, rated very high. She decided to try newspaper work, and has been happy in it and done well.

When there is a guidance counselor on the staff of the school which an Only attends, parents should certainly consult with him. If the school does not offer this service and the child or his parents are doubtful about what he should do, the principal may be able to refer them to a guidance clinic. The Psychological Corporation, 522 Fifth Ave., New York, N. Y., offers a full range of services. In general the fee at a clinic, including all necessary tests and conferences, will run to about $75.

Parents and youngsters who do not have the benefit of expert guidance can do a great deal by themselves to make sure that the youngster's choice of a vocation is wise.

The youngster's school record ought to be one of the best means of judging his general ability and his special interests. Parents of an Only must, however, realize that Onlies sometimes are given high marks not on the basis of ability but because teachers like their good manners and good behavior. However, a consistently good record, especially if it is achieved in hard courses in a school with high standards, is a sign of intelligence and so of the ability to do well in many fields. As in all guidance, comparative results may be the most informative. Again, a boy who has thought he wished to be a mechanical engineer but always does less well in mathematics than in other courses, ought to be shown that he might have a better chance in some other vocation where mathematics is not so important.

Advice is very different from domination, especially when a youngster is used to discussing problems with his family. If the parents do not feel qualified to advise, they can suggest that the youngster consult a neighbor or friend who has the necessary knowledge. But the best advice often requires no special information; it consists of helping a youngster to face facts. One of our distinguished Onlies grew up wanting to be a concert pianist. His family showed him that he was not nearly as good as Paderewski had been at the same age. They helped him see how few openings there were for second-raters. He says now, "They convinced me I should study law. I'm grateful to them. Music is my recreation but the law is my vocation and I love it."

Trial employment in the field in which a person expects to work may be extremely illuminating. One of our Onlies planned for years to be an astronomer. A summer's work in a university observatory made her decide she would rather teach mathematics.

Employment for Women

Girls are more likely than boys to drift into the first job that opens up. They expect to marry and may look on employment as just a temporary harbor. Many are never employed at all, but live on at home until they marry or until caring for their parents becomes a full-time job. We think a casual attitude toward employment is a mistake for any woman and a very great mistake for an Only.

Having a job one likes and is good at is certainly no detriment to matrimony. Regardless of the question of marriage, the better the individual is at her work, the more satisfaction she will have in it at the moment and the more security for the future. For the Only there are extra values in the contacts with other people which a job gives and in economic security.

An Only may be very vulnerable to ill chance because she has no close relatives in her generation. One of our Onlies, a college graduate, married soon after she took her degree. Within six years she lost her parents and her husband. She was left with a 4-year-old daughter to raise. She assumed she could step right into a teaching position but found that it would take a year to finish the courses in education required for her certificate. That year used up her slender resources and left her in debt. Another Only was given the custody of her two small children when she divorced her husband. She had been trained as a legal secretary, was able to find a job immediately, and was soon earning good money.

XV.

Sex and Marriage

"HE WAS the sweetest person in the world—to me and to everyone for the forty-five years I lived with him."

This comment on married life with an Only was made by the widow of an Only whom we had known particularly well. We and all of his host of friends agree with his wife's estimate. Nor was his sweetness the product of any lack of aggressiveness. He had been a famous athlete in college and the head of a great corporation. His life was a proof that Onlies can make good husbands.

We can cite case after case of Onlies who are good husbands and fathers or good wives and mothers. From our case histories and college groups, we have the records of 281 married Onlies. Of these, 24 have been divorced, but 14 of the 24 have remarried. None has been divorced more than once. Of the 295 marriages and remarriages, 524 children have already been born and the younger couples are still of an age to have children. These figures would seem to give the lie to the psychologist who said, "Onlies rarely marry and if they do marry they are impotent or refuse to have children."

What Research in Marriage Says about Onlies

A great deal of research is being directed at discovering the causes of marital unhappiness and divorce. Much of the research weighs Onliness amongst the many possible factors affecting happiness in marriage.

Terman rated 792 couples on marital happiness. Sixty-eight of the husbands and 99 of the wives were Onlies. The husbands who were Onlies and those who were married to wives who were Onlies rated as happy as the rest of the husbands. Wives who were Onlies or married to Onlies rated as slightly less happy than wives in general. Terman had but 8 cases of Onlies married to Onlies, and these couples had low happiness scores.

Burgess and Cottrell (*Predicting Success or Failure in Marriage*) rated 3566 couples on marital happiness. Of the 7132 individuals, 500 were Onlies. Of the 500, 108 were married to an oldest child, 189 to a middle child, 111 to a youngest, and 46 to another Only. Seventy-five per cent of the Only-Oldest combination rate as happy or very happy, 65.6 per cent of the Only-Middle combination, 59.4 per cent of the Only-Youngest, and 50.8 per cent of the Only-Only. The rating for all 3566 couples is 68.3 per cent. In a separate, more detailed study of 526 couples, Burgess and Cottrell found 55 husbands and 63 wives who were Onlies. Of the husbands 50.9 per cent rated fair to good in marital adjustment, and of the wives 61.9 per cent, compared with 71.5 per cent for all cases. Despite these less favorable percentages, Burgess and Cottrell do not think you can attach any weight to Onliness when you are trying to predict whether or not a person will be happy in marriage. When so many Onlies are happily married, the chances for a particular Only being happy or unhappy depend not on the fact of Onliness but on the individual's character.

Dr. C. W. Hall, in *Social and Educational Factors Related to Frequency of Divorce* (an unpublished Ph.D. dissertation, 1932, in the Yale University Library), compares the backgrounds of 300 divorced couples with those of 300 happily married couples. Thirteen of his happily married couples included an Only, as against 32 of his divorced couples.

Parents and Onlies need not be disturbed by these figures. The sensible point of view is: "Obviously a good many Onlies, like a good many non-Onlies, make a failure of marriage. But just as obviously, a great many make a success. What are the dangers that lead to failure and how can they be avoided? What are the steps to success?"

After studying our cases and comparing the facts which we have gathered with the findings of the experts about the components of a happy marriage, we must say that an only child who is brought up in accord with the principles advocated in our earlier chapters stands a very good chance of being happily married. All the authorities agree that a child who is loved and trusted, set a good example, disciplined reasonably but firmly and consistently, and helped to be independent and responsible generally grows up to be a good spouse. On the other hand, one who is overprotected, spoiled, and kept dependent is a poor marital risk.

The Oedipus Complex and Marriage

Some psychiatrists think that an Only may be a poor marital risk, because they believe that Onlies are more likely than non-Onlies to have difficulty in resolving the Oedipus complex.

Oedipus, it will be remembered, was the legendary king of Thebes who murdered his father and married his mother. The aptness of the phrase comes from the fact that Oedipus did not know what he was doing. His parents had been told that if they had a child he would bring disaster to his father and mother. So when Oedipus, their only child, was born they exposed him on a wild mountainside to die. He was found by a shepherd, who took him to Corinth, where he was brought up by the king of Corinth as his son. The young Oedipus heard a prophecy that he would murder his father and marry his mother, so, thinking the king of Corinth was his father, he went to Thebes and there unknowingly did just what he had hoped to avoid.

According to Freud, all children from a very early age are in love with the parent of the opposite sex and jealous of the parent of the same sex. Normally this love is redirected, sometime before the age of 6, to a sibling and somewhat later to an admired adult outside the family. In the teens the individual is ready to fall in love with a contemporary of the opposite sex. An Only, lacking a sibling to whom to attach his love and receiving the continued unbroken affection of his parent, may not make the normal shifts. He suffers, van Krevelen says, from the Oedipus complex in its purest form.

According to Freudian theory, the Oedipus complex is unconscious, but nonetheless, if it is not resolved, if the normal shifts are not made, the complex remains a potent force in determining the individual's behavior. It may, for example, make it impossible for the person with an unresolved complex to marry, or at least to marry anyone but a person strongly resembling the loved parent. In the latter case, the consummation of love may give rise to feelings of guilt and may directly or indirectly wreck the marriage.

Van Krevelen and Winnicott agree that it is not impossible for an Only to resolve the Oedipus complex. But Winnicott says that in later life the only child is likely to be found "at home with the parent of the opposite sex, the parent of the same sex being dead or content to play second fiddle." Van Krevelen says that the only child "is bound ever closer to his parents to the point of fixation." He states that this close attachment is most probable in the cases of the only son of a widow or the only daughter of a widower. He says that more only daughters than only sons marry because during the crucial years (up to the age of 6) the mother is around a child more than the father.

Our case materials give some support to van Krevelen's conclusion. Twenty per cent of our men Onlies of marriageable age are unmarried. This is higher than the percentage of unmarried men in the general population. And our women Onlies seem at least as likely to marry as women non-Onlies.

A few of our unmarried men seem to be too devoted to their mothers. For example, one middle-aged son of a widow is still a bachelor. He had excellent legal training and was doing well at the bar. But when his father died he gave up his profession. He lives in his mother's house and he and she go everywhere and do everything together. If an invitation does not include them both it is regretted.

But most of our case histories of unmarried men and women Onlies seem to show other reasons than attachment to the parent of the opposite sex as the probable cause of failure to marry. Many of these Onlies are taking full care of both parents and so have obligations which hinder their marrying. The histories of our unmarried women Onlies are very similar to those of hosts of unmarried non-Onlies: study at a women's college, immediately followed by absorption in a career, like teaching, where opportunities to meet eligible men of the right age are, or at least have been, relatively scarce.

A small number of our histories show difficulties in courtship and early marriage that can be traced to the overattachment of a parent of the opposite sex to an Only or vice versa. One woman reports, "My father hated my fiancé and made it just as hard as he could for us to get married. But here we are and are happy." Another says, "My father didn't like me to have boy friends. I could go visiting, but not if there were boys in the family. The result was I was always on the lookout for a man. But I broke down when my father died, and ended by marrying a man a good deal older than I am." An Only divorced from an Only says, "I married a man who was also an Only, due to loss of an older brother. He had a doting mother. It would have made no difference whether I was the girl or not—she would have liked no one he married." Another Only lived with her parents until both died, and then, at the age of 37, married a much older man, "like her father, even to his mustache." Her father had been considerably older than her mother.

When there is any evidence that marital unhappiness is due to a lingering attachment of either spouse to a parent, the individual needs professional treatment. Psychiatrists cite many cases where such people have been helped to work through their difficulties and have turned out to be good spouses and good parents. There is some evidence that difficulties may disappear after the death of the parent involved or after divorce and remarriage, but a great deal of misery can be avoided if a psychiatrist is consulted early. It is still better, of course, for parents to bring up their children in ways which minimize the danger of too close a tie, conscious or unconscious, to either parent. Both parents should take a share in bringing up a child, thus affording ample opportunity for the child to identify with the parent of the same sex. Children should be encouraged to make friends with children of the opposite sex, expecially in their teens. As the years go on, they should be given independence and responsibility in full measure and should be encouraged to look ahead to marrying and raising a family of their own.

Homosexuality

A tendency to homosexuality, produced either by an "Oedipus constellation" or by dependence on the parent of the same sex, is often attributed to Onlies. There are many cases of homosexual Onlies in psychiatric literature, but, as far as we can find out, no reliable comparative study has yet been made which proves that Onlies have an unusual tendency to homosexuality. Levy found no homosexuality among his cases of maternal overprotection. On the contrary, he says, their heterosexual adjustment was "successful, and also early [because of] their refusal to forego any pleasurable pursuit." In our group of Onlies there are but two known homosexuals, both men. One of these appears to have been very dependent on his father, the other on his mother.

The Problem of Homosexuality, by Karl M. Bowman and Bernice Engle, is both a thorough treatment of what is known about homosexuality and an excellent guide to normal sexual development. Bowman and Engle's recommendations largely coincide with those we have just made. In particular, they urge the desirability of youngsters' association with children of the opposite sex, especially during their teens. They point out that more men than women are overt homosexuals, and therefore stress the desirability of a father's taking a full share in bringing up his son. The boy then "has a man to identify with and a beloved mother figure to possess as an ideal."

Sex Education

Authorities on marriage say that full and accurate information about sex, preferably obtained from parents or teachers before the age of 18, shows a high correlation with happy marriage. Sexual ignorance and sex information obtained from "the gang" show a high correlation with unhappy marriage and with divorce. But there are many exceptions in both directions. When both partners to a marriage have accurate sex knowledge, early and good sexual adjustment is promoted. But good sexual adjustment is no guaranty of happy marriage, and initial sexual ignorance is not usually a permanent impediment to sexual adjustment.

We have, however, some reports from Onlies who say that at marriage they were abysmally ignorant of the anatomy of the opposite sex, of the mechanics of sexual intercourse, and even of the physiology of reproduction. And we have reports from parents of Onlies who are obviously not giving their children the benefit of a good sex education. Of course, non-Onlies as well as Onlies often lack proper sex education, even when their parents are determined that the children shall have the best possible academic education. Fry found that practically all of the Yale students who consulted him about sex were superstitious and meagerly, even falsely, informed. Many of them merely needed information. They were not abnormal or promiscuous, but puzzled and confused.

One Only remembers: "My parents told me nothing. A friend, also an Only, and I used to have long discussions about 'sex.' She had an amazing collection of old wives' tales that I swallowed as truth. In my teens I made a frantic but vain search of dictionaries and encyclopaedias. I was afraid each time I kissed my fiancé that I'd get pregnant."

A parent of a 6-year-old Only reports: "She wanted a kitten, but we hadn't given her one. One night when I was putting her to bed she asked, 'Mother, do kittens lay eggs?' I was afraid of what might come next and (I guess you'll think I'm foolish) said, 'I don't know.' 'But where do little kittens come from?' 'Oh, Mary, I don't know. Go to sleep.' 'Mother, don't you know anything?' "

All children ask questions as casually as this. If they are answered directly and simply—"Kittens grow in the mother cat"—the child is satisfied. As he grows older he will ask more-and-more-detailed questions and can be given more-factual answers. In this way he gradually acquires accurate information suitable to his age level. But if the parent consistently fails to answer questions, the child senses evasion and embarrassment and stops questioning his parents. He goes elsewhere for his information, and develops a guilty feeling in connection with sex, as well as getting a lot of queer ideas. A parent who has trouble answering a young child's questions will find a great deal of practical help in Sidonie Matsner Gruenberg's book *The Wonderful Story of How You Were Born.* There are several other good books, including *The Wonder of Life,* by Milton Levine and Jean Seligmann (for children 6 – 10), and *Attaining Manhood* and *Attaining Womanhood,* by George W. Corner (for teen-age boys and girls). Your public librarian will be able to recommend still others, some written for parents and some for children.

Children with brothers and sisters learn about the anatomical differences between the sexes before there is any question of modesty or of embarrassment. The Only may be at a distinct disadvantage in this respect. If children are "shielded" too long they may suffer from strange phantasies or become persistent Peeping Toms. There are several easy means of avoiding such ignorance. If from the time the child is a baby he sometimes sees his parents nude, he will eventually notice differences, ask questions, and be given simple answers. (The questions will be repeated from time to time as he grows older.) But when a child has not been brought up in such a casual atmosphere, it would be a mistake for the parents suddenly to let him see either of them naked. The older child might be shocked. The child would be more aware of how he or she differed from the parent of the same sex, e.g., in breasts and pubic hair, and perhaps disturbed by these differences as well as by the differences between the sexes. And parents who have been careful to be fully clothed in the child's presence probably couldn't change their habits without embarrassment.

Some mothers of very young Onlies arrange with friends to have "bathing parties." The Only then can have his bath with a child of the opposite sex and about the same age. Somewhat older children can be given the chance to help bathe a neighbor's baby. If opportunities like these are taken advantage of with any regularity, the child grows up without being self-conscious. This does not mean that he will not develop a sense of modesty. Boys and girls, however accustomed they may have been to nudity as children, become personally modest at about the time of puberty. Their inclinations should be respected.

A child who has a pair of pets and breeds them learns about anatomical differences, intercourse, and reproduction in a very natural way. If his parents are interested in the pets too, he will naturally consult them. This is an excellent opportunity to be sure that his sex education is satisfactory and that he has not been misled into believing ill-informed friends.

Educational films are also an excellent means of teaching a child about differences in anatomy and about the process of reproduction. The University of Oregon Medical School, Portland, Oregon, has issued a film for 6-year-olds, *Human Beginnings,* and one for junior- and senior-high-school students, *Human Growth.* These films can usually be secured free of charge from state departments of health. Parents can arrange to have them shown to church or school groups or to groups organized by Mothers Clubs. A pamphlet, *The Gift of Life,* has been prepared by the New York State Board of Health to accompany the films. Parents whose child sees the films should try to secure a copy of the pamphlet as an aid in follow-up. It's particularly useful in helping children learn the proper terms to use. Catholic, Jewish, and Protestant clergymen collaborated with the editors of the pamphlet and approved it in its final form.

How objective children can be about sex is shown by the reaction of a 10-year-old Only, a girl, to *Human Growth.* She had seen the film at a meeting of boys and girls and their parents, which had been organized by a Mothers Club with the help of a specialist from the state board of health. The night the film was shown, a girl friend of about her

age was staying at her house. The two girls got ready for
bed and then wandered into the mother's room. They pulled
up their nightdresses, pointed to their navels, and asked,
"Is this where the cord was?" They were much more interested in themselves than in what boys were like.

Why Don't I Have Brothers and Sisters?

"Why don't I have brothers and sisters?" is one question
that parents of an Only have to answer sooner or later.
We've asked about fifty mothers how they answer this question. Their comments show that children, particularly
younger children, will accept any straightforward, unhesitat-
ing answer and apparently forget about it. The largest number of these parents told their children something like "God
hasn't seen fit to give us another." One parent added, "You
must make up the difference to us by having lots of playmates." (This same report went on, "As often as possible
we have playmates for lunch, picnics, etc., to help develop
personality.") A goodly number of the parents start their
reports by saying, "I told him the truth." The added explanations vary from a simple "I couldn't have any more"
to "I was too old to have any more" and "I have a fibroid
that will prevent me having any more." One child asked,
"Is it possible for people *not* to have babies if they don't
want them?" The mother writes, "And, in all honesty, I did
say, 'It is possible to prevent having them,' and that seemed
enough at the moment."

We feel that in general it is better to tell the child the
truth than to evade a question, but the truth can be kept
very simple. A young child should not be burdened with
anatomical information or terminology which he cannot
understand. Explanations, especially those given to young
children, should not imply either fear of childbirth or unwillingness to have more children. An adult Only reports, "I
remember resenting the fact that my mother never had any

more children, even though she explained she was getting rather old to have children when I was born and was afraid to have any more." A 7-year-old whom we know may be building up a similar feeling. She asked one of us, "Do you know where babies come from?" She immediately pointed to her tummy, and added, "My mother can't afford the time to have another baby." In both these cases, a plain, "I can't have any more," might have worked better, at least for the time being.

The Danger from Perverts

Parents of Onlies sometimes restrict the child's activities severely because they are afraid of perverts. There are an unfortunate number of child-molesters, but the danger has been greatly exaggerated. Miami, Florida, which, as a resort city, would be likely to be a congregating point for perverts, has about twenty arrests each year. There are undoubtedly more cases but probably not many more, because the true pervert, being abnormal, is likely to repeat an action until he is caught. Many molester-hunts are started by a child's seeing an entirely innocent man urinate by the roadside. When neighborhoods are excited by rumors of an exhibitionist, parents can take comfort in Kinsey's conclusion that "exhibitionists are rarely rapists."

The hunting grounds of perverts are the streets leading to and from schools. Every child should be warned never to accept candy or gifts from strangers, and never to accept a ride from a stranger. If a stranger offers him a ride, he should write down the license number of the car (using a stick to scratch it in the dirt if necessary) and report it to his parents. Parents should report all suspicious cases and all available information to the police. They should urge judges to commit known cases to an institution for treatment, instead of merely ordering them out of town as too many judges do.

A child's questions about perversion should be answered as simply as is consistent with the truth. One 10-year-old Only, who had heard her mother talking to a friend on the telephone about the arrest of a high-school student accused of homosexuality and also about a local election, asked, "Mother, what did Johnnie do?" "You know," the mother said, "I've told you that if anyone touches you in the movies you should get up and go out. Johnnie was touching boys in a way he shouldn't." The minute this short explanation was finished, the child asked, "Who won the election?"

Parental Example

"Onlies," writes one of our Onlies, "observe their parents' marital behavior more than non-Onlies because they have no brothers and sisters to distract their attention. If the parents are happily married, the Only has the desire to be happily married, too, and strives harder to make marriage a success."

Despert, in *Children of Divorce*, puts the matter more specifically. She says, "The best education of children for sexual love in marriage derives from the healthy sexual relationship between their parents. It is in the climate of the parents' satisfaction with each other that children find their own growth toward happiness in sexual love. Here they learn at its source the joyful emotional approach to sex which makes the techniques of sexual satisfaction easy to achieve after marriage."

It's a lot easier to say, "Set a good example," than it is to follow that advice, but perhaps parents will try especially hard if they have a look at the reverse of the picture. The evil influence of parents' disharmony on the marriages of their children has been observed by all students of marriage. Our case histories and Hall's research confirm the fact that divorce is particularly common among Onlies whose parents have been divorced. This result is probably partly due to the bad effects on the Onlies' sex adjustment of a poor parental example, and partly to the personality difficulties which result when a child grows up in an atmosphere of emotional strain. Moreover, the example of divorce is in itself a danger. Almost every marriage has its crises. A young husband or wife whose parents have been unable to solve their difficulties may, when trouble comes, say, "Well, this is it," and give up very easily. There has been an unconscious expectation that trouble would come and an idea that the way to get out of trouble was to get a divorce.

Parents who are still trying to dominate their child even after marriage increase the probability that the child will run away from not-impossible situations. The child is used to turning to the parents when in trouble, and they are used to taking the child's side. When a child marries, parents should redouble their efforts to encourage independence. They should certainly discourage the young couple from living with them or even near them. They should avoid all suspicion of interference.

Looking Forward to Marriage

Onlies often ask if they have a fair chance of having children and of being good parents.

In our studies of Vassar and Mount Holyoke graduates, we found that married Onlies have, on the average, a somewhat smaller number of children than do non-Onlies. This is due to the higher percentage of marriages of Onlies which have no children, and this in turn is largely due to a tendency of Onlies to marry late. About the same percentage of Onlies as of non-Onlies have an only child.

Our general impression is that these comparisons hold true for all Onlies as a group. Other studies have shown that there is a slight tendency for low fertility to run in families, but that this does not preclude great differences in generations. We have one Only who has ten children, one who has nine, two who have eight, and several who have five or six.

By and large our Onlies have made good parents. Their comments on their difficulties show that these are the usual run of problems. Some say that they find it very hard to put up with and to control their children's fighting. Some say their own sex education was very inadequate and that they have difficulty in telling their children about sex. Some, that they tend to reverse the way their parents treated them: to be too easy-going if their parents were dominating, too strict if their parents were permissive. There seems nothing in these complaints that an intelligent young couple, duly forewarned, could not overcome. And the majority seem to us, judging them professionally, to be doing a pretty good job.

The chances of being a good husband or wife and a good parent can be greatly increased if the young people concerned will do some hard thinking and study ahead of time.

The first and most important factor in making a marriage work is, as Kinsey points out, a determination to make it work. If you are an Only you have to be prepared for being accused—even by your spouse—of being selfish, self-centered, and in general spoiled. You have to be determined that you will not behave in ways that will lend substance to these accusations.

You must realize that marriage is not the continuing honeymoon that certain romanticists have pictured. When young people are first in love they are blinded to each other's shortcomings. A habit that seems "cute" during courtship can be deadly irritating after a few months of married life. A special hazard for an Only is the expectation of remaining the center of the stage, of being waited upon.

There's a pertinent paragraph in the Government pamphlet *Your Child from 6 to 12.* "Polly's father, calling her his little sweetheart and shelling out money whenever she coaxes him, is not setting up a very good pattern in her little-girl mind as to what to expect from men. It would be unfortunate if she were to grow up to be a little-girl woman, and expect always to be on the receiving end."

Marriage is a sharing, and sharing should extend into all phases of life. One of our distinguished Onlies, who is separated from his wife, says, "Things might have been different if I had realized at the time that she thought she wasn't any help to me in my work." Separate plans and pleasures may very soon result in separate bed and board.

There is a wise old saying, amply confirmed by modern research, that the most successful marriages are based on "passion, companionship, and respect," but that with any two of these a marriage can be made happy. Too often, young people marry on the basis of passion alone. They are sexually attracted to each other and do not take time to find out whether they can respect and like each other too. Statistics show that an engagement of about six months often precedes a happy marriage. This gives the young couple a chance to explore each other's interests and to be aware of what habits either has that irritate the other. If the handicaps are too great, the engagement will not last. Breaking an engagement requires a good deal of courage but it's a lot easier than divorce.

There are marriage-counseling bureaus in many cities. These bureaus make a specialty of advising young people before marriage. Your Family Welfare Society will be able to tell you if there is such a service readily available to you. If there is, take advantage of it. In the meantime, and in any case, you should read a book like *Building a Successful Marriage,* by Judson T. and Mary G. Landis. This will help you realize both the problems and the rewards of marriage in all kinds of matters from sex relations to budgeting. Then it is up to you to see what your own special problems and assets may be, and to set out to solve the former and to make the most of the latter. Good luck!

XVI.

How About Another Child?

"SHOULD we have another child?" "What's the best interval between children?" "What can we do to ensure having more children?"

These are among the questions young parents with an only child ask most frequently.

We feel that, if circumstances are favorable, it is a mistake to limit a family to one child. We think being an Only is hard on a child. We think that parents who love each other and like children are missing a great deal in life if they have only one child. We think that parents who are deliberately limiting themselves to a single child should review their reasons with open minds.

The Cost of Children

In the Milbank Fund survey of Indianapolis, two thirds of the 365 one-child couples in the sample stated that economic reasons were a factor in their not having a second child. About half of these 365 said that economic reasons had influenced their decision more than a little.

The parents' standard of living bears directly on the number of children they feel they can afford. Many who think they can give one, but not two, "every advantage," or at least the advantages which they themselves have enjoyed, limit their family to one. For example, college graduates who have not been financially successful tend to have smaller families than their more successful classmates. A survey of Harvard, Yale, and Princeton graduates disclosed that the men who are financially the most successful average 2.17 children per man, the least successful 1.28.

We do not know any formula which parents can apply to let them know how many children they can afford. We are reminded of a conversation between a mother of four and a mother of one. Said the mother of the Only, "We can't afford more than one child and I don't see how you can." The mother of four replied, "Since you press me, we decided that we couldn't afford an Only." (We must add that the Only and the four have all turned out very well!)

The high cost of education, particularly a college education, is one of the main economic deterrents to having more than one child. Current all-inclusive costs of a college education vary from a low of $700 a year in state or municipal institutions to $2000 and more in the leading women's colleges. The total of $3000 to $10,000 for four years (plus much more if graduate work in law or medicine follows) is enough to stagger even well-to-do parents. But parents should remember that growing up with brothers and sisters is good education, too. If plans are made far ahead, if the children will earn something toward their own education, and if they will try to do well enough in their studies to win some scholarship aid, the eventual gain for each child may very well exceed the gain of an Only whose education is presented to him on a silver platter.

Fear of a Second Pregnancy

The Milbank Fund survey indicated that the wife's poor health was the second most frequent reason against having another child. Sixty per cent of the 365 one-child couples in the sample said that the wife's poor health had somewhat influenced them against having a second child, and 55 per cent that it had influenced them more than a little.

Our own case histories show that much Onliness is due to fear of a second pregnancy. The wife or the husband or both may think that the wife is not well enough to risk having another child.

Whether or not it is desirable and safe for a woman to have a second child is a question that no one but a specialist familiar with the details of a case can decide. Parents should be on their guard against jumping to conclusions.

We asked three leading obstetricians how often they had told a mother of one child that she shouldn't have another. The replies were identical: "Almost never."

One obstetrician writes: "The commonest deterrent to a second child as I see it is a long, moderately hard first labor that seems much worse to the woman and her husband than it really is. It isn't a real physical deterrent but she makes it a deterrent for emotional reasons. Some who have the first by Caesarean are so scared they never want to try again. Some are professional women doing some interesting work they don't want interrupted. Some seem to get everything they want from their first child and center *very much* on it. Of course there are a few cases who can't have more. One had her first pregnancy at 40 (luckily twins) and had trouble with blood pressure. Infection (now rare with penicillin), toxemia, heart trouble, tuberculosis, diabetes, severe asthma would keep some women from subsequent births."

The three obstetricians agree that second births are generally easier than first. They also agree that, when a couple feel they would like a second child, a difficult first labor should not stand in the way.

The Best Spacing

There are many theories and few facts about the best spacing of children. There are cases of every interval from the minimum to the maximum which have worked out well, and many which have worked out badly. Certainly the obstetrician should be asked for advice as to what is physically best for the mother.

Many parents (when health is not a matter of special concern) think close spacing is most convenient. Some psychologists see advantages for the children when they are within two or three years of each other: there is less jealousy (though a 2- or 3-year-old can suffer keenly from jealousy) and more companionship. Some psychiatrists feel strongly that the second child should come when the first is still less than 5 years old, because the new baby helps the older resolve his Oedipus complex. Winnicott says of a first child who is 5 or more when the second is born that throughout life "any rival in his love affairs, in his business, in his career will arouse the intensest antagonism in him." Gesell, however, says, "Current theories have exaggerated the dangers of a jealousy reaction toward the arrival of a new baby." He also says, "Usually the 3-year-old child is becoming psychologically ready to make a good adjustment to a new baby."

The Almost Only

Planned or accidental spacing of offspring may result in what we call an "almost Only": the child who is raised as an Only until he is 5 or more, or the child who is much younger than the other children. Other almost Onlies are the only boy or girl in a family, and the child who is an Only because of the death of a sibling. In each of these situations there are dangers which may aggravate or be aggravated by the dangers inherent in Onliness. Oldest children are notoriously prone to jealousy and selfishness. An oldest child who has been the sole center of attention for five or more years is more aware than a younger child would be of the way a new baby weakens his position. The one child of a favored sex, especially the boy who arrives after a series of girls, is in great danger of being spoiled and of learning to look on himself as superior. A child who is much the youngest in the family is also in special danger of spoiling and of overprotection as well. A child who is an Only because of the death of a sibling is quite likely to be overprotected. His parents may be terrified at the possibility of losing him, too. They may feel guilty because they wish it had been this child that had died instead of the other, and compensate for their guilt by trying all the harder to keep him safe.

After one of these situations has come to pass, there may be nothing the parents can do to change the facts. But they can do a great deal to prevent any ill effects on the child if they will be alert to mistaken attitudes in themselves and if they will deliberately try to foster independence and responsibility in the child.

Fertility

"We waited and waited and nothing happened."

We've heard these words so many times in response to our question, "Why Only?" that we are convinced that the parents of the majority of our Onlies would have had more children if they could have. Perhaps they might have been more successful had they realized the significance of having to wait and sought professional advice promptly.

Our studies indicate that, on the average, mothers of only children are two years older at marriage than are mothers of two or more children and that, on the average, they are four years older at the birth of the Only than other mothers are at the births of their first children. The older the mother and the longer the interval between marriage and the birth of the child, the more likely the child is to be an Only. Our analysis of the vital statistics of Vassar graduates shows that 78 per cent of the mothers of two or more children and 58 per cent of the mothers of Onlies conceive within two years of marriage. Other investigators have found that in the case of normally fertile couples the wife usually conceives the first child within one year after marriage or after ceasing to exercise controls.

If there is to be a second child, he generally comes along pretty quickly. Our Vassar figures show 72 per cent of second births within three years and 83 per cent within four years. Another investigator found that 60 per cent of the women who had had one child and were trying to have another conceived again within three months, and 90 per cent within one year.

If, then, a mother wants a second child and has not conceived after six or eight months of trying, she and her husband should ask their family doctor to recommend a fertility specialist. Early consultation is especially advisable when either the husband or the wife comes from a small family and when either is over thirty years old. Fertility decreases markedly after thirty—more than half of our Onlies were born to mothers over thirty—and there is no time to be lost.

XVII.

Planning for Old Age

YOU may be startled to be told that planning for old age is part of your job of bringing up an Only. But one of the first facts that struck us as we analyzed our case histories of adult Onlies was the large number of Onlies who had had to care or were caring for one or both parents. A closer study of these histories showed that the Only had often made enormous sacrifices in order to ease the old age of a parent, and that too often these sacrifices had been in vain. Neither the parent nor the Only was as happy as both might have been with more careful early planning.

Here is a typical case—one of many. Joan had a very happy childhood. She did well in high school, and showed a particular talent in her course in commercial art. She went from high school to a local junior college that offered courses in display advertising. Her father, a traveling salesman, was glad to have her attend the local college, both because it was cheaper and because she would be at home to keep her mother company. As soon as she graduated, Joan got a job in a local advertising firm, and continued to live at home. Men were attentive to her, but she did not take any of them seriously. She had her job, and after hours she had her mother to look after. Then her mother had a stroke. Joan's father's salary, even combined with her own, didn't stretch to cover the nursing care that was necessary. Joan gave up her job and took on the duties of twenty-four-hour nursing. It was exhausting work, but three nurses would have had to be paid three times as much as she earned. Her mother died, after ten years of being bedridden. That very year, Joan's father was retired at the age of 65 and came home to live. Joan had to get a job to eke out his income, but by now she couldn't compete in her chosen field of art, so she took a clerical job. Her father lived another fifteen years, and died when he was 80 and Joan 50. She still has her clerical work, but is not very happy at it. And she's wondering what's going to happen to her if she loses her job or even if she keeps it until she is retired at 65. She has no savings. And Social Security will hardly do more than pay rent for one room.

Onlies like Joan are very cheerful about their sacrifices. They don't see what else they could have done. But occasionally we hear a story full of bitterness. Alma told us: "My mother was sick for years. I taught school all day, rushed home, took care of her all night, and dragged myself back to school next morning. Her illness used up all of our resources. When my mother died, I was so near a breakdown, I had to stay out of school to recuperate. I'm still in debt. I've never been myself since."

We are sure that the mother of another Only, an Only who arrived as a happy surprise after the mother was 40, was not foreseeing a picture like Joan's or Alma's when she said, "A baby is a lot of work, but I'm glad to take care of her because she'll take care of me when I am old."

Most parents are willing to make any sacrifice for a child when the child is young. They do not mean to ask a child to sacrifice himself in return. But if the parents do not plan for their old age they may, before the end, require their child to sacrifice a career, love, and a chance for children.

The Right Attitude

If you are a man of 45 today, you can look forward to living until you are 71. If you are a woman of 45, you can expect to live until you are 75. If you have a child of 15, the chances are that you will live to see your child as old as you are now and in the prime of life. Will his life be as full as yours now is, or will he have sacrificed his career and a home of his own to care for you?

If you are looking ahead and hoping to keep from being a burden on your child, it's a good idea to examine your attitude. Do you really think of the child as an individual and not just an extension of yourself? Do you agree that "parents have no rights but many responsibilities?" Are you expecting your child to lead an independent life?

The other day we heard of parents giving their only child, an 11-year-old girl, a mahogany desk as a birthday present. The girl is at the age where she likes secrets, even from her parents. She was therefore delighted to find that the desk had drawers that could be locked. "Can I keep it locked?" she asked. "You certainly can!" "And hide the key?" "Any place you like." "And it's really all my own?" "It certainly is—it's yours now and you can take it with you wherever you go: to college, to the town where you work, to your own home when you get married."

As your child grows older, he will have to make many decisions that may be swayed by your attitude. If you have the right attitude, you will not be governed by what would be pleasant and convenient and financially economical for you, but by what is best for him.

Separate Households

When your Only starts in his first full-time job, encourage him to take an apartment with a friend and set up housekeeping for himself. This may seem very foolish at the time, particularly in the case of a young man. A mother is going to say: "Will he have the right food? Who will darn his socks? Think of all he can save if he lives with us; he'll have all of his salary clear."

The most frequent argument against separation is the financial one. The Only can live more cheaply at home than in a separate establishment. Many parents even use their purse strings to take the place of apron strings and keep their Only safely tied to home. When this is done, the Only resents both having to stay at home and the method of holding him. In the long run it would be better for both the child and the parents if all concerned did with less money in order to have more independence.

We are convinced that most of our men and women Onlies who are unmarried and living in the household with their parents first found it convenient to live at home, and then easy not to marry. Then suddenly they found that they were responsible for the care of an elderly parent and it was too late to change. On the other hand, our Onlies whose parents urged, or at least did not oppose, an early break have in general married happily. A few have not married, but they *and their parents* have led happy lives.

The great majority of elderly couples in the United States have managed to maintain separate households. And only one quarter of the elderly widowers and one half of the elderly widows are living with relatives. But our case histories show that of the elderly parents of our Onlies, three fifths of the widowers and four fifths of the widows are living with their Only. No less than 73 per cent of our unmarried Onlies of marriageable age have a father or mother living with them.

It may shock the sentimentalist, but other investigations and our case histories show that elderly people prefer to live independently and that members of the second generation who have the day-by-day care of elderly parents are often resentful and unhappy. Since both generations are happier living apart, both should plan their lives on that basis.

If you are convinced that you should live apart from your

Only when he grows up, you ought to start planning for your separate dwellings immediately. The sooner you plan, the more likely you are to have your mind set for independent living and so to avoid drifting into a joint household.

Parents of ordinary means have to plan far ahead to finance their own home and perhaps to help the young people finance theirs. An expanded Social Security program may make this easier to do in the future, but savings will still be important. All opportunities for saving should be explored. For example, it may be well to encourage an Only to earn and save money toward his college education so that the parents may save that much toward their old age.

As soon as an Only begins to live apart from his parents, the parents should consider whether or not they wish to keep their present quarters. A move may make large savings possible. And moving when one is still comparatively young may be much less of an emotional strain than it would be five or ten years or more later.

We have one case of unwillingness to move that is tragic in itself and typical of many. A couple had continued to live on in their big house after their only child moved to a distant city. The child died when they were in their sixties. The husband died at 65. The expenses connected with the two deaths left the widow very little, but she refused suggestions that she move into an apartment. Within four years of her husband's death she owed $500 for groceries and $400 for back taxes. She had to apply for Old Age Assistance. With that she can eke out a living, but she is more and more alone because she hates to face her friends or to have them see the way she lives. She worries because she cannot keep the house in repair. She has given up her hobby of oil painting because she cannot afford materials. She doesn't even think of selling her antiques. She's living in social isolation surrounded by the physical symbols of a better past.

The Kind of Place You Will Need

One couple in their forties were planning a new house, but in the meantime living in a second-story, walk-up apartment. They invited older friends in for supper one night but were told, "We'd love to come, but we can't. Jerry has a bad heart, and the doctor says he must not climb stairs." So the younger couple changed their plans and built a one-story house for their old age, one without a flight of steps in it.

When you make a move it should be into quarters that are small, planned for easy cleaning, and equipped with labor-saving devices. There should be a minimum of stairs that have to be climbed. A two-story house or an upper-story apartment should have an elevator. Easy-to-get-out-of bathtubs, nonslip floors, fire-safety, and good lighting are other desirables. If you are building, ask your architect to plan your house for your nineties. You will want a place for your child, grandchildren, or great-grandchildren to sleep when they come visiting, but not necessarily extra rooms. If you have storage space you can keep a roll-away bed there, and the sofa can always serve in an emergency. You'll live longer and so see more of your descendants if you don't take on too much to care for.

Communities especially planned for older people deserve consideration when you are about to move. Some cities are building housing projects which will make provision for a percentage of older couples and single people as well as for younger people. Friends of ours, a couple in their nineties, have bought into a private community and are finding life there convenient and enjoyable. Their purchase price includes a sort of insurance arrangement that will care for them the rest of their lives.

Keep Your Social Contacts and Make New Ones

Just as a rich social life on the parents' part is a safeguard against their concentrating too much attention on their child when he is young, so continuing social contacts help prevent their clamping down on him when they grow old. If you are not careful you will find yourself more and more alone as you grow older. Some of your lifelong friends move to other towns. Some become deaf or blind or crippled and tend to cut themselves off from you. Many die. When none are left, you may be entirely dependent on your Only and his friends. This can make a lot of trouble.

If you are going to make new friends and keep old ones, you must always be ready to go more than halfway. You have to be willing to telephone, to call, to suggest meetings and activities. If a friend is bedridden, make it your business to go to see him regularly. If one is deaf and unable to hear the rapid-fire conversation of a group, make a chance to see him alone and retail to him the best bits of gossip and some of the bright remarks.

When there are not many of your contemporaries available, you can help fill the gaps by increasing your contacts with younger people. In fact, the earlier you start to make young friends of your own, the better. Young people like occasional contacts with older people for whom they are not responsible. One of the big advantages of having a place of your own is that you can entertain young people and not feel that you are interfering with your Only's friendships. Try to find out what some of your young acquaintances like to eat—and drink—and throw a party once in a while. If you can keep up your bridge or poker skill, even though you may be no genius, they'll like to come and play with you now and then. Make an occasional survey of your assets. What have you that younger people would like to share for an afternoon or an evening? One old lady we know has the tennis court on her place kept up for the young neighbors. We can't all own tennis courts or swimming pools, but a good cigar can be bait.

Keep up your part in community and church activities of all kinds. Younger people naturally take over the offices and the planning, but they are glad to have the help of older people to telephone to a long list of people or to address a thousand envelopes. If you belong to a card club or social group, do your best to keep the club active. Insist that younger people be taken in as the old ones drop out. Some day you will be the grand old man or the *grande dame* of the group and it will be sweet.

When You Must Live with Your Child

If you are already living in the household with your Only or if circumstances force you to do so in the future, there are many things that can be done to ease tensions and to make life happy for the whole family.

Parents living with a grown-up Only find it very hard to remember that the son or daughter is no longer a child. This is particularly true if most of the money for running the house is provided by the parent, but it is also true when the major income belongs to the Only. As far as money is concerned, some sort of budget and working agreement is essential. We do not recommend that you turn any capital funds you may have over to your Only. Too many old people have done this and, like King Lear, lived to regret it. We do recommend that each member of the household knows and agrees on who pays what for what. An unemployed Only keeping house for a parent ought to be paid a definite wage and no questions asked about how it is spent. An older person who begins to feel incompetent should ask a bank's advice about how to manage and allot his funds.

You as the parent should try not to dominate the household. In effect, positions are now reversed or soon will be. Your child, of whom you took care so long, is now taking care of you. He has the right to the authority and responsibility which you once exercised, just as you still have the right to your independence. The Only is now an adult, legally and morally responsible for his own behavior. He may heed your advice if you interfere, but he may hate you at the same time.

Three Generations Together

If you have grandchildren in the house, you have to be more than ever careful not to interfere. You can be a big help, but you can be a big problem, too. We once collected several hundred papers from school children who wrote on the topic, "My Major Problem at Home Is ————." A large number of these papers completed the title by adding "Grandfather" or "Grandmother" and proceeded to tell about having to keep quiet, or get in by a certain hour, or not bring home guests, "all to keep the peace with grandma," as one child put it. The standards which the young couple set for their children and the methods of discipline which they use are entirely their responsibility. If you interfere, you cause enough friction to start a conflagration, and you don't improve the youngsters' behavior.

Remember too that your grandchildren's first allegiance is due their own parents. One common trouble in households containing three generations is that the grandparent becomes a rival for a child's affections and tries to win the child over by spoiling him. We've known this to result in some pretty sorry specimens of children, and we've seen it alienate one or both of the middle generation.

You and everyone else will be much happier if you can have your own private room with a private bath. Having your own stationery, magazines, newspapers, radio, and even a TV separate from the household's also helps to avoid friction and outright quarrels. You can watch the wrestling match while your grandson listens to his symphony. If he prefers your program he can come to your room as your guest and you can send him out when you wish.

We hope you have a family council and that you have a seat on it. If you brought your child up on the council system, both of you are ready to continue. If your family hasn't had a council, try suggesting one.

There are many problems in a joint household but many compensations, too. You as the older have less loneliness and perhaps more security. You have ready-made contacts with the world. If you are cheerful and willing and understanding, you can help in many ways—practically, by baby-sitting or cooking or cleaning, and emotionally, by being an always-available, always-loving listener.

Occupations

"The well-earned rest" featured in the illustrations of insurance advertisements is a delusion and a snare. No one wants to fish all day long every day, even if the fish do bite. And they don't. The happiest old people are people with regular occupations—working in their usual job or self-employed or running a household or absorbed in a hobby. As Dr. William Burnham said, three things are necessary for healthy living, "a task and a plan and freedom to carry them out."

Find out long in advance what your employer's retirement policies are. If you can keep at work by accepting a change in duties, do not let pride interfere. If there is a fixed retirement age, don't think your company will make an exception for you. Plan ahead to retire at that age into some other work that will keep you happily occupied.

We have some splendid success stories of shifts made by people over 65. A psychologist became the country's leading specialist in advising old people. A bank treasurer became head of a loan company, a business man undertook library research, and a company executive became a star salesman. Few people over 65, however, get new jobs that are more lucrative or even more interesting than their former jobs. Usually it is necessary to drop down the scale—perhaps like the piano tuner who applied his knowledge of tightening wires to tightening barbed-wire fences. We know a retired teacher who became her town's most popular baby sitter.

Vocational-counseling services are now beginning to help older people who wish to find continuing work. Sometimes, by means of tests and interviews, they can uncover possibilities of which the oldster had never dreamed. Ask your Family Welfare Society if there is such a service in your locality. If there is a "retraining school" in your company or in your community, take advantage of it.

If you can't get paid work that takes your full time or any time at all, you ought to see if there is any volunteer work at which you would be good. Ask your Community Chest secretary what organizations need volunteers. You may find that there is a regular training course for volunteers. If so, take it.

Hobbies are a great resource whatever your age and whatever your employment, and they are an ever-present help as you grow older and have time on your hands. If you are still a mere 50 or 60, make a start on a hobby that you can ride when you are no longer able to walk.

The greatest opportunity to keep busy and useful may be right in your own home. Our favorite father of an Only was retired, much against his will, from his job as a factory superintendent. He was then 80. His daughter had more than a full-time job teaching and writing. He promptly took over all the housework—ordering meals, cooking them, washing dishes, and even, in a masculine fashion, cleaning. He became proficient, and more, at his job. His angel cakes are famous through two states. He's now 87, and very lame from arthritis, but still going strong. He has his tasks and makes his plans, and his daughter doesn't interfere. They are a happy household.

Geriatrics

Much can be done to keep yourself healthy, physically and mentally. Your attitude is important. Your aim should not be to live forever but to live as full, happy, and useful a life as you can. You must be willing to do your part in keeping yourself fit. This requires some knowledge of the difficulties which you face, willingness to seek out and accept the best advice available, and a determination not to quit.

Regular medical examinations, preferably at least once each year, are the best way to forestall the crippling illnesses of old age. Doctors can't yet cure cancer, heart disease, and cerebral hemorrhages—the main causes of illness in the aged—but, if given time, they can do much to prevent them or at least to minimize the effects. The years between 40 and 60 are the critical time. If you are in that period, you probably feel pretty well, and probably are pretty well. But see your doctor just the same.

Good medical service is expensive, especially if it requires hospitalization. One of the characteristic worries of old people today is about how to meet their doctors' bills. Fewer than one in four have health or hospitalization insurance. You should join a well-organized plan that will keep you a member for life—and you should join as soon as you can.

Mental Health and Hygiene

Minds, like muscles, need exercise to stay in the best possible condition. Older men and women can continue to use their minds at a high level in the absence of disease affecting the blood vessels which supply the brain. There is some loss of intelligence, but there is a great increase in experience and in judgment. The ability to learn may slow down, but it remains present to a remarkable degree. Memory of recent events is not as good as in younger people. But both learning of new material and memory of recent events are excellent when the individual is really interested, pays attention, and means to remember and to use the new information. And these are just the conditions which promote thorough learning in a teen-ager! Creative activity remains possible and more than possible. There are hosts of elderly people who are doing good creative work in such fields as education, sociology—and gerontology.

Cicero, who wrote a still-valuable essay "On Old Age," makes a great point of citing examples of old men who continued to be active and useful. *The New York Times* recently had an article about some of our current leaders who are well along in years, including Churchill, Baruch, Einstein, Maugham, and Adenauer. Few of us can be as famous as this, but we can keep sound minds even while our bodies grow feeble if we keep intellectually active and satisfy our emotional needs for security, affection, recognition, and new experiences.

Clinging to the past, being hidebound in a routine, and disliking change are all habits which speed the aging process. The more you look backward, the faster you go downhill. The antidotes are to do some intellectual and creative work every day, to keep informed about what is going on in the world, especially in your lines of major interest, and to try to do some things which relate you to the future. When King Cyrus the Great was an old man, says Cicero, people were astonished to see him planting acorns. Why did he, when he couldn't live to see the trees? His answer was, "For the benefit of generations yet unborn."

XVIII.

Caring for an Elderly Person— A Parent or Yourself

THE previous chapter was written for the parents of an Only. This chapter is written for the Only. Perhaps both generations will read both chapters and be able to discuss them objectively. We feel that a frank discussion of the problems we take up would be of particular value between an Only who is anywhere from 16 to 40 years old and a parent who is anywhere from 35 to 65. A distressing number of Onlies and their parents let matters drift until too late.

Early Independence

It is important for you to establish your own career, your own living quarters, and your own family in the early years of your maturity. If you are still in school or college, plan now to make the break when you take your first full-time position. If you postpone matters, you are more than likely to find it too late. One of your parents may die, or both become ill. They will be accustomed to depending on you. You cannot desert them, nor will you wish to. But if the break is made early there is a better chance that they will have made satisfactory arrangements for independent living. Even if circumstances are such that you must later take your parents to live with you, you and they will be better off if you have had a period on your own. Perhaps reading these chapters will give you the courage to make your own declaration of independence.

A Parent's Remarriage

"I've told our son Jack that if his father marries a cross-eyed, one-legged woman a month after I die and Jack doesn't accept her with complete equanimity, I will haunt him for the rest of his life."

More than one young adult has interfered to prevent a parent's remarriage and lived to regret it. Our civilization places a premium on married life. Older people, like younger people, fit in best when, to use a good old-fashioned word, they have helpmates. The statistics show very clearly that elderly couples maintain their independence more often than do elderly widows or widowers. If you prevent a remarriage, you are depriving your parent of his best chance to find continued happiness and usefulness.

A parent's plans to marry again may shock a grown-up child. Remarriage seems disloyal to the parent who has died. The young adult, whether married or single, may look on it, with its implication of renewed sex life, as somehow obscene. But, whether the young person recognizes the fact or not, the principal feeling against a parent's remarriage is usually a matter of finances. There is a fear of immediate curtailment of financial support and of ultimate loss of all or part of an expected inheritance.

Our materials contain some pertinent accounts both of fights over a remarriage and also of successful remarriages which have worked to the advantage of all concerned. One daughter broke up her father's engagement "because Mother hadn't been dead a year," but he later married another woman, who does not seem to the family friends to be as fine a person. Some parents who have yielded to pressure not to remarry are living on with their children. The old people apparently harbor a resentment which complicates a situation that isn't easy under the best of circumstances. On the other hand, one of our Onlies writes: "My stepmother is just a little older than I am. She was a widow with a daughter about my son's age. She made my father very happy for twenty years. She was and is everything the sister I never had could have been to me, and her daughter is like a daughter to me."

Typical Cases

Our records are full of two types of history. In one, the Only continues to live at home and gradually takes over increasing responsibility for managing the family affairs. In the other, the Only makes a break but no one has developed an adequate plan for the parents' old age. In this case, the Only often sacrifices some or all of the start he has made in his chosen work and takes up the burden. Here are two examples.

Mary Jones graduated from college and got a job teaching in her home town. She "naturally" lived on with her parents. Her father was a distinguished and delightful person. He encouraged Mary in her work, and made it possible for her to travel. She had many good friends. Her father died when he was 80, his wife 75, and Mary 40. Mary's mother immediately proved to be a difficult person. She was stubborn in resisting suggestions, suspicious of Mary's handling of money matters, and jealous of Mary's friends. She hated every hour she had to stay alone but refused to pay for a companion. Mary's mother had never gone out much, and after her husband's death went out not at all. She became practically housebound. For fifteen years Mary's life was a routine of early breakfast, hurrying to school, hurrying home, and hurrying to shop and cook and clean. Her reward was suspicion and complaints and the knowledge of a duty done. She behaved well, but she was often bitterly rebellious.

Donald Dawson was brought up on a Vermont farm by overage parents. His mother was 40 and his father 45 when he was born. He went through college and medical school and began practice in Washington, D. C. He married, and he and his wife lived in a small apartment. Before Donald was making much of an income, his mother died. Neither the family doctor in Vermont nor Donald had any special knowledge of gerontology. All they could think of for Donald's 80-year-old father was to have Donald and his wife take him to live with them in Washington. The old man missed his farm and his animals and his old neighbors. Donald's wife found the old man underfoot all day long. Everyone might have been far happier if arrangements had been made for Donald's father to live on in his own neighborhood, perhaps boarding in a farmer's family and doing what he could to help the farmer.

These cases are typical of what can happen when adequate plans are not made in time. But if you find yourself, gladly or unwillingly, in a similar situation, it does no good to say what might have been. You and your parent have to make the best of matters. Here are some things you can do to help your parent keep up his part.

Finances

Less than one fifth of the people who reach 65 have resources which make them financially independent. If your parent will not be able to support himself and pay the heavy medical expenses which almost surely will come, you have to plan to help out. Our records suggest that unmarried daughters are most likely to suffer when their parents' finances prove inadequate. The daughter stays at home to care for her old people. When sickness uses up their funds she is too old to start work. We feel strongly that every only daughter should be trained to earn a living and that every unmarried only daughter should get a job as soon as she can and keep it. Even if it turns out that the extra money is not needed, she has the advantage of outside contacts.

Old people usually deteriorate in their numerical ability sooner than in other abilities. They have increasing difficulty in keeping accounts, writing checks, and balancing a checkbook. They may lose bills, receipts, and deposit slips. They may refuse to believe they have not paid some bills but pay other bills twice.

You may find it necessary to arrange for a bank to manage a parent's financial affairs, including collecting income and paying bills. Another arrangement that has worked well is to have two accounts, one a joint account in your name and your parent's, the other a separate account in your name alone. In that way you can control the amount of funds at your parent's disposal. You can keep the joint account low and so protect yourself against his drawing out all your money while letting him feel as though he had funds to spend. Don't leave your parent without any money. To be without money of his own would humiliate him, and it might speed up the tendency to depend on you for every kind of service and decision.

Occupations for the Elderly

You know from what we have said earlier how much having something to do helps the morale and even the physical well-being of an elderly person. Yet you may, out of mistaken kindness or false pride, prevent your parent's finding jobs to do. You may say, "We don't need the money, why don't you take it easy?" You may think caning the neighbor's chairs is beneath the dignity of a man who once managed five hundred employees. When an older man, or even woman, starts to help around the house you may say, "Now you sit still and let me do it."

Instead of encouraging an older person to relax in idleness, you ought to encourage one who tries to find things to do, either paid employment or volunteer activities or household tasks. The main things to remember are to *praise publicly and repeatedly* anything the individual does well, to *make clear that you have been helped* by what he does, either by the money or by the time saved, and to *let the individual do the job his own way.*

Sometimes elderly people propose plans that are obviously beyond their capacities. If you hear your parent dreaming up a grandiose scheme, don't interfere until you must. He will probably end by cutting the cloth to fit his figure or by doing nothing. In the meantime, he's had a pleasant dream. But you may find that you have to be firm about keeping him from starting something which you know he cannot finish and which would involve you in heavy expenses or even in a great deal of extra work. Even in routine daily tasks you may have to pitch in and finish—or clean up— something an elderly person has begun and found too complicated or too exhausting. Nevertheless you should let him go on trying when there is any chance of success. He may sometimes go to sleep while dinner is cooking and let it burn, or stumble and drop a box of eggs. Such minor tragedies will be a price paid for keeping him going. They are outweighed a thousandfold by his gains in independence and in cheerfulness.

Social Contacts

You may find that you have to take a good deal of initiative in helping an elderly person make and keep social contacts. Invite his friends in to have meals or to watch TV with him, even if you don't personally like the people he likes. Keep out of the way as much as possible, and don't dominate the conversation if you are sitting with them.

You'll quickly find which of your own friends get on well with your parent and which ignore him or are even rude. Some of the latter may have more care of the elderly than

they can take at home, and some may still be resenting the
way they were brought up and therefore be unsympathetic
to parents in general. Don't blame them, and don't give
them up as friends—you must, above all, keep your own
social contacts active—but don't try to have your parent
mix with them on social occasions. When you find friends
of yours who like your parent, plan to invite them in frequently. Be sure your parent knows who is coming. Tell him
some time ahead, and again just before they arrive so that
he will remember their names and be looking glad to see
them. Arrange the seating so that he can take a real part in
the conversation. An occasion when your friends are with
the two of you is a good time for you to praise him for
something he has done that you really like. Point out the
well-weeded garden. The friends will add their own com-
pliments, and he will receive the recognition he needs. Be
equally mindful not to mention any of his mistakes, however jokingly.

An elderly parent is prone to be extremely critical even
of his own friends and of your friends who are nice to him.
This may be an attempt to reassure himself that he is superior, or it may be jealousy of the attention the friends receive
from you. You must not let such criticisms interfere with
your efforts to keep your social life vigorous.

Patience, Objectivity, Good Humor, and Affection

You are going to need all the virtues in the book to live
cheerfully and happily with an aging person. You have to
learn to protect yourself. Your biggest safeguard is to realize that there is nothing personal in your parent's attitude.
A good geriatrician can help you understand why character
changes as we grow older, and, though he may not be able
to prescribe any alleviating drug for your parent, he can at
least help you to be more objective. You must recognize that
even into old age we are all likely to harbor lingering re-

sentments against parental authority. You may be inclined to work yours out against your parent, and he his against you. So, if you have an occasional spat, don't blame yourself. Try to laugh at yourself as soon as you can.

An occasional vacation from each other's company is essential for both your parent and you. If you can afford it and he is physically able, insist that he spend a couple of weeks twice a year at a resort hotel. Try to take a separate vacation yourself in addition to those he takes. You may have to employ a nurse to take your place while you are gone, and he may object violently to having a "baby sitter." But if he can't take care of himself, you should insist on some such arrangement. The important thing is to get away.

You'll need a few real breaks every day. One of our Onlies says, "I can't be too thankful that we have a yard big enough for me to have a garden and that when I'm in the garden my mother knows I can't hear her. I don't think I could take it if I didn't have an hour or two a day to myself by myself." Another Only pays a neighbor's teen-age son to read aloud to his mother twice a week. Another snatches a few minutes to herself when the Visiting Nurse comes to give treatments. If you can arrange your absences so that they follow a fixed schedule, the older person learns to accept them, and even to put up with a sitter if one is needed.

When your parent is ill, it is wise to take care of him in the home as long as possible. There are not yet enough good institutions planned to care for elderly patients and to rehabilitate them if possible, though we hope there will be some day. But it is unwise for an Only to assume entire care of a chronic invalid, and most emphatically unwise for one to give up a job to do this if any other arrangement is possible. When the Only can no longer manage the necessary care or secure the desired help, institutionalization is advisable. This is especially true in the case of senile patients, like the parent of one of our Onlies who kept wandering away from home if not watched day and night.

The decision to commit a parent to an institution falls very heavily on an Only. When a parent has several children, they share responsibility and give each other courage. The Only often has to act alone, and, if he has been devoting his whole life to the care of the parent, faces desolate emptiness after the commitment. This is a time when warm friendly relations with your doctor, your lawyer, and your bank's officials are of incalculable assistance. These people are all accustomed to cases like yours. They can be both sympathetic and matter-of-fact in their advice. They will know what should be done and how to do it.

Your Own Old Age

Many of our Onlies are now well advanced in years and are living full, happy lives. The arrangements they have made vary enormously. One wealthy old couple maintain two homes, travel extensively, and are very much the social arbiters of two hotels in which they spend regular vacations. One old lady of 86 began years ago to take young men as boarders: two of a long succession still live with her; they are a spry 60 and look after her as though she were their only child. Several of our elderly Onlies are still actively employed, at least part time, and living in their own households. Some are living in church homes or in convents which make a business of boarding single people of all ages. One or two are well cared for in foster homes of their own choosing.

You may find it hard to realize that you will soon be having to solve for yourself the problems we have been discussing. The prospect of growing old alone may terrify you so much that you refuse to think about it. But if you have always been mentally healthy there is nothing to fear in old age, provided you lay your plans wisely. The main thing is not to delude yourself with the idea, "I won't live that long." Face the future courageously, cheerfully, and objectively. Keep up with the literature on gerontology and geriatrics. Plan to keep busy and to be useful.

XIX.

The Personality of the Only Child

OUR case histories indicate that the great majority of only children grow up to be well-adjusted adults. They have jobs that they like. They are happily married and raising families. They are taking an active part in the social life of their communities and bearing their fair share of public duties. These are signs of a healthy personality.

There is evidence in our materials and in those of other investigators that Onlies do not achieve their success without a struggle. This struggle may of itself be valuable. People who overcome handicaps grow strong in the process. But there is always the danger that an obstacle will prove insurmountable. Certainly parents will not deliberately put obstacles in a child's way. They will want to lend a helping hand when they should. Even when they must stand aside as spectators, they will want to encourage and applaud.

The experiences of parents of Onlies and of Onlies themselves point to some things which it is important for parents to do and some which they should not do. These have been discussed in detail in earlier chapters. We sum them up here.

Love, Security, Recognition

Every human being needs to be loved and to love, to feel secure, and to be recognized as somebody in his own right. Good adjustment depends on the way these needs are satisfied. Love can smother as well as inspire. A child can be kept so safe that he is timid and fearful. He can be praised when he has not earned praise, and so be kept from making the real effort on which recognition should depend. An only child, because he may be so much the center of his parents' life, is vulnerable in all of these ways.

Parental Example

A child learns many of his ways of adjusting to life by watching how his parents live. Parents who love each other implant in the child's mind an ideal toward which he will strive. If they have many friends whose company they enjoy, he grows up a friendly sympathetic person. If they set high standards for themselves and work hard to achieve them, he sees the joy of persistent effort as well as the rewards of success. Affectionate, sociable, energetic parents satisfy their child's emotional needs without surfeiting him.

Father's Part

A boy Only needs the fun of doing many things with his father. When a warm companionship exists between father and son, the son models himself on the father and learns to be a man. If the father does not do his part, the boy, brought up in the matriarchies of the modern home and school, has no help in his struggle against effeminacy. To the girl Only, the father must be father and brother, too. But a father should not monopolize his daughter's time; she needs to learn from her mother a woman's way in the world.

The Security of Discipline

Parents who discipline their child with firmness and consistency build a solid foundation for his development. Knowing what he must not do makes him feel safe in trying what he can do. He sees that there is more than one way of looking at things and that he must govern his actions by what others want as well as by his own wishes. He learns to wait, to share, and to work. Thus he wins support and approval, and his feeling of security grows. He becomes strong enough to be generous in all his human relations.

A Gregarious Animal

"We are not only gregarious animals, liking to be in sight of our fellows, but we have an innate propensity to get ourselves noticed, and noticed favorably, by our kind." William James, the father of American psychology, wrote these words in 1892. They are everlastingly true.

Three forces tend to separate an only child from his fellows and so to deprive him of the chance to win their recognition. He lacks brothers and sisters to accustom him to being with people and to make contacts for him. His first association with other children may be such a shock that he avoids them as much as he can. His parents may monopolize his time to the exclusion of potential friends.

School affords the only child an automatic opportunity to make friends. Starting in nursery school, where many of the other children are also Onlies, is a big advantage, and kindergarten ought to be compulsory. Parents must provide their child with out-of-school playmates of both sexes. An Only should be encouraged in his friendships. His home should be open to his friends, and he and they should be free to come and go and act their age.

Responsible Independence

The months-old baby can be seen trying to do things for and by himself. A wise provision of nature starts him preparing to stand on his own feet long before he is ready to walk alone. If a baby were not allowed to creep and crawl and pull himself erect—and fall—his muscles would not be strong enough to support him when the time came for him to stand up. When parents are so centered on their child that they do everything for him, he is helplessly weak in crises.

Youngsters learn independence and responsibility through experience. Learning by doing is nowhere more valid. School, camp, and college take the boy or girl away from home for hours or months. They are the proving ground of his ability to care for himself. But life at home, if it is not hedged about with restrictions, is the training ground where a child learns to act independently for himself and responsibly for others. Some time to play alone, chores, and hobbies all help him find out how to plan and how to carry out a plan with a minimum of dependence on others.

Life as an Adult

Perhaps no choice is without consequences, but two seem fateful. What vocation? Whom to marry?

Everyone would like to be both happy and useful in his life's work. The vocational-guidance expert sums this up in the phrase, "work in line with the individual's abilities and interests." When a young person's abilities and interests are discovered in the teens or before, there is time to try them out and to secure the best possible training. He needs his parents' advice and help, but the final decision is his.

When a responsible person marries it is with a full sense of the obligations entailed. The spoiled person marries to gratify himself. An Only who has loved and been loved by happy parents and brought up to be independent and responsible succeeds in marriage as in the rest of life.

The Will and the Way

No life is devoid of strain and stress. There is no parent but wonders—sometimes if he is doing right, often if he could not have done better for his children. No child matures without experiencing pain and conflict.

The mentally healthy person adjusts to the strains of life. He recognizes his problems and does his best to solve them. He is not too blind or too proud to seek help in time of need. Conscious of having done his best and of his willingness to try his best and to adjust to circumstances, he does not worry unduly.

The problems which an only child faces are essentially those faced by all human beings. Onliness is at most a complicating factor. Sometimes it makes a problem more difficult of solution. Not seldom it smooths the way. Parents who view life objectively and, recognizing present and possible difficulties, apply intelligence and common sense to overcome them, can feel confidence in the future of an only child. The child himself, as he matures, need have no regrets that he is an Only. The values of life are the same for all—he as well as anyone can achieve them if he will.

Index